THE

EMPOWERED CHILD

How to Help Your Child
Cope, Communicate, and Conquer Bullying

DANIELLE MATTHEW, LMFT

Publishing Services provided by Paper Raven Books
Printed in the United States of America
First Printing, 2017

Hardback ISBN = 978-0-9994075-0-9
Paperback ISBN = 978-0-9994075-1-6

*This book is dedicated to Pam,
for always believing in me and helping me to find my way to my
passion.*

Table Of Contents

Note to the Reader

I have written this book for you, a parent of a child who is experiencing bullying. For 20 years and counting, every day in my family therapy practice, I work with children just like yours—children who are wounded, hurting, and just wanting someone to help them make it all better. It is my deepest wish that this book helps you and your child, right where you are.

I'd like to take just a few sentences to prepare you for a few things that you might notice in this book.

First, rather than using a clumsy "s/he" pronoun, I have consistently interchanged the pronouns so that when I'm speaking to you about "your child," I will sometimes use "she" and sometimes use "he." Please, recognize that I'm referring to your child, regardless of gender.

Second, I have included two terms that are typical in psychological practice but may be unfamiliar to you: "**empath**" and "**empathic**." In the psychology world, "**empaths**" are sensitive to others' thoughts and feelings. Throughout this book, I'm going to encourage you and show you how to be "empathic," that is, to be sensitive to your child's thoughts and feelings.

Third, the children and families shared in this book are a combination of real and hypothetical examples, with names changed to protect privacy. The names chosen are, indeed, stereotypically "American." I don't want to distract the core principles I'll be sharing with a hypothetical name that's particular to a culture. The principles, here, work in all familial and cultural contexts, even if they look different. So, please try not to dwell on the names of the children discussed in this book.

And, finally, I will be showing the child's perspective, as much as possible. As a therapist, I see how many problems arise because adults simply don't see and hear what they're children are saying, even as much as they desperately want to. When you read how I describe that a parent reacted harshly or angrily to their child, please know that I *know* it will be frustrating for you to read these parts of the story. But, I also know that you want to change how you interact with your child. That's why you're reading this book. If you and I can be honest with how we're reacting to our children, only then will we be vulnerable enough to admit that we can be more vulnerable, more honest, and more *empathic* with our children, so that we can help our children to cope, communicate, and conquer bullying.

Thank you for sharing your journey with me,

Danielle Matthew, LMFT

Foreword

My wife and I lost our eleven-year-old only son to suicide, due to bullying. I can attest to the unbearable pain and devastation that bullying can and does cause, not only to the victim of bullying, but also to the ones that love the bullied child.

After losing our son, my wife Laura and I could not bear the thought of allowing this to happen to another child, another family. It became our life's mission to stop bullying in this world. We founded an organization called Stand For the Silent, and we now travel around the world, raising awareness around the epidemic of bullying, spreading a message of love, and supporting the need for legislative change concerning bullying.

In recent years, with the use of social media growing, bullying has increased to epic proportions. More than 160,000 kids miss school every day because they fear being bullied. One out of every four children will actually have planned how they would take their own life before they graduate from high school.

Suicide has become the second leading cause of death in our young people ages 10 to 24 years old, second only to car wrecks.

Sadly, these staggering statistics are not just numbers. They are people. People who we know, people who we love. People like my son.

Far too often we hear the words, "boys will be boys," or, "bullying is just a rite of childhood passage, it's just something all kids have to go through." As adults, we may remember being bullied when we were young and think, "I got through it," but bullying has changed since then. With the advances in technology, bullying has become a whole different ugliness.

But it doesn't have to be this way! The good news among this darkness though is that there is help available to stop it. Learning to empathize with the victim of bullying is crucial to being able to help them. Only when we can feel their pain and devastation, can we help them heal and empower them.

I first spoke with Ms. Matthew when she attended a school presentation I was giving in California. On that day, I found a like soul who was as passionate as I, to end bullying and save lives of children in this world. I've had the opportunity to see the work she does to raise awareness and to combat this growing problem of bullying. Danielle's tireless work in her practice and within the following pages have shown me that we—parents, educators, therapists, people who care—can give our children the skills they need to cope, communicate, and conquer bullying.

This book will show you how to tell if your child is being bullied, how to reach out to those being bullied, and how to have a conversation about bullying with both the bullied and the bully. It will teach you how to heal from the wounds that bullying causes and how to rebuild confidence and self-esteem, coping skills, and empowerment, but more than all of this … it brings hope. Hope for a brighter future for the young people of our world, a future without bullying.

Read this book, learn from it, and teach our kids the practices it contains, and together we can overcome bullying, help heal those that have been bullied, and empower our children to rise above this and stand strong for themselves and others.

I personally have spoken to over 1,275 schools around the world and well over 1,375,000 kids. I've seen the practices that Danielle teaches work time and time again. I am thrilled to see this wonderful resource become available to our fight to end bullying and its life changing consequences. The tools it contains are valuable to us all.

Kirk Smalley
President and co-founder
Standforthesilent.org

Prologue

In the fourth grade, I was bullied for the first time.

My mother and father were divorced, and I lived primarily with my mother. My mom and I had just moved into a new apartment, and I was attending a new school. Starting over was a very daunting task for a chunky little girl who had been put back a grade due to a learning disability.

In the beginning, I really enjoyed school. I engaged with the teachers, I played in the yard with my group of girlfriends, and we had playdates after school. I opened up my heart to these girls, trusting them to be my friends and confiding some of my most personal feelings about moving to a new school and my learning disability. I let them see my vulnerabilities. I thought they were truly friends I could trust.

But within a year, the girls who had once been my friends, who had played with me after school, started giving me the cold shoulder. The ringleader, with her shiny hair and perfect freckles, the girl everyone in the group looked up to, started a game of "ditch." The girls would come close to me, pretending to be friends, and then run away, laughing at me.

Why had these girls, who had once been my friends, suddenly decide to pick on me for no apparent reason? They made me feel like I was the class joke. Within a few days, I'd lost all of my friends. I remember coming home to my mother, tears running down my face, and telling her how mean the other girls were to me. I felt horrible about myself.

My mother would offer me daily encouragement, urging me to just ignore the other girls, to not let them see how they'd gotten to me. My mother was patient in her direction, even suggesting I confront the girls directly, on my own. But though my mother was coming from a loving place and truly wanted to help me deal with the bullying, I still felt very alone in my sadness. I felt like I had no friends, like I was all alone.

There was something my mother didn't know, something that would have allowed me to leave my pain behind and not carry it with me into adulthood.

I've written this book to share that something with you.

Introduction

In my lectures on bullying, I always tell people that it's important to have just one true champion who loves us, who will go out on a limb for us, and whose behavior toward us will never be influenced by what others say. The importance of having that one connection, that person who really gets you, is the key to surviving childhood.

If you have a child who is dealing with a bullying situation, you know your child is hurting. You talk with other parents. You watch the news. You know that children who are bullied can become anti-social, depressed, and suicidal. You panic.

You don't want to think such a drastic ending could be possible for your child, but you're so worried that you can't control the dark places your mind races to. You don't really even know whether your child is being bullied, or whether the bullying has stopped. And your child may not want to talk to you about the bullying—a life-threatening silence.

Too often, parents don't learn about bullying until it has reached a crisis point. Kids do not want to tell their parents what is going on. Parents aren't always tuned into social media where their children might post pleas for help, or wishes for self-harm.

In this book, I want to give you tools to use so you won't be the last to learn about your child being bullied. And I want you to feel capable of managing the bullying, while respecting and openly communicating with your child. I'm going to introduce you to a framework that I use in my own therapy practice. I call it the "Three Es," and the Es stand for **empathy**, **empowerment**, and **engagement**. You can start a conversation with your child using empathy to help your child feel safe and heard. Then, you can then seek to empower your child to create a plan of action to cope with the bullying. And, finally, you can help to engage your child in carrying out that plan of action, providing support along the way. I will explain each of these Three Es and how to use them, but know that if you can make a habit of using the Three Es as you help your child deal with a bullying situation, you will be a true champion for your child.

Throughout this book, I will provide you with clear strategies and ideas so you feel you can open a dialogue with your child and talk to him or her effectively about bullying.

I think back on the little fourth-grade girl I was, ditched by her friends and teased every day. Even today, I carry the pain of my bullying wherever I go. I want you to have a better roadmap to handling bullying with your children. I don't want any children to feel so alone, to feel there is nobody who can help them. I hope that the little girl I was can now use her own experiences to lead parents down a different path that can be empowering for both you and your child.

Chapter 1:
The Basics of Bullying

———➤◄———

"**Bullying**" is a word that many people use to describe how another person treats someone. The term is often overused, and a one-time fight between two equals is often described as bullying. In fact, this is a form of "**conflict**." A single fight between two teenagers, for example, is not bullying, as both kids have contributed to the issue.

The true definition of **bullying** is a persistent pattern of behavior in which someone enforces power over another person, through the threat or use of verbal, physical, or relational violence. If one teenager has power over another and is physically aggressive on a regular basis, that would be considered bullying. The bully holds power, repeatedly and in patterned ways, over a perceived weaker person, chosen because the bully believes that person will have a hard time standing up to him or her.

If we misuse the term "bullying" so that it encompasses a broader (and less serious) range of adolescent and childhood behaviors, then we are in danger of failing to properly address a very serious issue, one which could have potentially disastrous consequences. There is a true bullying epidemic as described by a World Health Organization statistic, which found that within the 12 years of school, a child has a 70% chance of becoming involved in bullying, either as a bully, a victim, or both.

If children who are bullied are not properly treated, their feelings of depression and hopelessness can get worse. Their depression can become so extreme to the point that they may think of suicide. Nowadays, kids may ask for help by putting their story on YouTube or social media, or texting their feelings of helplessness to their friends. If these messages are caught soon enough, then help can be given to these victims of bullying. However, there are many times, as we hear about too often on social media, when it is too late. The message is not caught. Kids feel they can no longer live and do end up committing suicide.

Four types of bullying

There are four main types of bullying that a child may face.

The first is the most well-known: **physical bullying**. This includes hitting, kicking, punching, or tripping another person. Physical bullying is easy to see so adults can intervene much more quickly than they can with other types of bullying.

Verbal bullying is also common and includes name-calling and making mean comments to someone's face. This type of bullying again is easy to hear, so it can be easy to address.

In the past 15-20 years, with the development of the Internet, **cyberbullying** has been on the rise. People can now post mean comments on social media or impersonate other people. Cyberbullying is bullying that takes place using electronic technology and includes phone calls, text messages, emails, social media posts, blogs, and creating fake websites in someone else's name.[1] The scope of cyberbullying changes as fast as our technologies change, which means it is not easy to detect or even stop. When the mean-spirited information goes out into the abyss, you cannot delete it; the data lives on.

A final type of bullying that seems to be receiving more attention is **relational bullying**. This is ostracizing a person, leaving her out, gossiping, or spreading rumors. Relational bullying is mostly common in girls. A great resource for middle school girls is called "Stories of Us."[2] These are films created by middle school girls about middle school girl issues. One video has a great depiction and understanding of relational bullying.

The movie starts with two girls spreading a rumor in home economics class about whether another girl really is pregnant. In the next scene, the girl is shown coming up to the other two who were gossiping about her. She explains that the rumor is untrue. The two gossiping girls look at each other, say they understand it's not true, but then slowly turn their backs on the girl anyway. They further ignore her until she walks away.

This is a textbook example of relational bullying. In this case, the bullies are sneaky and flying under the radar, making it very difficult for adults to catch them.

---

1   http://www.stopbullying.gov/
2   http://www.storiesofus.com/

Why are some kids bullied and not others?

We may have cultural stereotypes about kids with glasses or knobby knees being picked on, but in truth, there is not one typical person who is more likely to get bullied. However, we can identify certain factors that play into someone being bullied.

The kids who are usually the targets of bullying are any kids that bullies feel may have a potential weakness. This weakness could be only in the bully's eyes, but it is usually a difference that others have difficulty accepting. Sexual orientation, some form of disability, physical appearance and ability, social awareness, and socioeconomic status are just a few examples of the types of differences that bullies prey upon.

For kids, being different is a hard concept to understand. As adults, we can embrace differences in others. We can enjoy learning about people who have experienced different lives and different challenges. However, most kids have a hard time accepting differences.

For example, children who are on the autism spectrum tend to relate to others differently. This group of children can be bullied because they may be different in their responses and interactions. This also goes for children who have special needs, are exploring their identities, come from a different racial, cultural, or religious background, or simply enjoy experimenting with their physical appearance. There are basic norms and ideas that society puts out about what is acceptable and what is not. The role of social norms plays a huge role in who is targeted by bullies. Any child (and, truth be told, adult) perceived as different may be greatly affected by bullying.

I had one client, Jeremy, who had been verbally and physically bullied for years. During the first few sessions with me, he would describe the bullying with tears in his eyes and repeatedly state that he had just accepted that the bullying was part of his life. I realized that he had been beaten down for so long by others that he felt powerless. He truly felt that the bully had won. He believed he could really do nothing to change the pattern of behavior. Jeremy had begun to believe the bully's harsh words, internalizing them to the point that he felt both helpless and hopeless. He felt that nothing would get better and he should accept how others treated him.

Jeremy's parents and I began to build him back up, and I will describe that process in the next chapter, but sometimes the reason people are bullied is simply because they have been bullied in the past. When a child starts to accept bullying as a fact of life, things really start to become dangerous, and we need to come in to help before our child's mental state deteriorates.

How can I tell if my child is being bullied?

As a parent, it is not always easy to detect whether your child is being bullied. 64% of children who are bullied do not report it, and children do not report bullying for many reasons:

- They want to handle it themselves.
- They don't want to get their parents involved.
- They don't want their parents to think they can't handle their own problems.
- They don't want to be considered a "snitch."

- They're embarrassed.[3]

There are some important signs to pay attention to that will help you determine whether your child is being bullied. Look for a pattern of behavior.

If your child is suddenly more isolated and does not want to come out of her room, this may be a sign of bullying. Your child may have engaged well with the family previously and now wants to be alone all the time.

Another sign may be a decline in grades. If your child was previously a good student and involved in many social activities, but is now isolating themselves in his room on a regular basis and there has been a decline in grades, this may be a reason to worry.

You should also look out for signs of depression. If your child has low moods, had previously been outgoing and is no longer having friends over or going to others' homes, this may also be a reason to be concerned.

Body language can vary for kids who are being bullied. Some kids are hunched over and look depressed and some have their heads down on a desk or pillow, while others' body language may appear scared and fearful.

These are strong indicators of bullying and should be monitored. If there are signs that you observe and you are concerned, it is important to seek further help immediately for your child.

---

3   Bradshaw, C.P., Sawyer, A.L., & O'Brennan, L.M. (2007). Bullying and peer victimization at school: Perceptual differences between students and school staff. School Psychology Review, 36(3), 361-382.

Your reaction to your child's bullying sets the tone for possibilities

It's hard to ask parents not to be upset or angry when they find out that their child is being bullied. Some parents will tell their child it is fine to retaliate because they want their child to send a clear message to the bully that he or she will never hurt their child again. Or, they are angry at their child for being, in their eyes, weak.

Children do not want to tell their parents because they are afraid of **re-victimization**. At a most basic level, if a child "tells" on a bully, that bully might retaliate with increased bullying. But, what most parents don't consider is that children also sidestep telling their parents because they fear the reaction of their own parents. Though unknowingly, parents who learn that their child is being bullied often subject that child to reliving the bullying when their own strong emotions come into play. A story of Jeremy, a client I worked with, will offer a good way to show how your reaction affects your child.

Jeremy waited a long time to even tell his parents about the bullying he was experiencing, and when he finally did, his parents weren't prepared to be fully emotionally supportive. Within a few weeks after they'd discovered that Jeremy was being bullied, his parents brought Jeremy to work with me.

For our first session all together, we sat in chairs, arranged in a circle in my office. I listened to their words and their tone. The words Jeremey's parents chose were supportive, and yet their tone sounded angry and clearly frustrated. He sat there, with tears in his eyes. I saw first-hand that Jeremy felt re-victimized. It was not done purposely. Jeremy's parents were simply overwhelmed and said the first things that came to their minds: "How could you let this happen?" and "Why did you not tell us earlier?" But when these questions were asked in a harsh tone of voice, with hands thrown up in the air and eyes rolling, Jeremy felt hurt for not speaking up.

Children tend to not want to burden their own parents or make them feel angry. I could only imagine how badly Jeremy felt, and yet my heart went out to the entire family. All they wanted was for the bullying to stop.

But simply wanting the bullying to stop and jumping straight into problem-solving mode actually prevents your child from sharing his emotions.

Despite their best intentions to help their son, Jeremy's parents were so focused on the shock of finding out the bullying was still going on, that they weren't actually listening to Jeremy.

Put your child first

Instead of reacting in a way that makes your child's problem worse—remember, she is the one suffering the torment of bullying first hand. Be ready to take care of your child the way she needs. I have worked with many kids who feel hopeless and helpless. They feel disempowered by being bullied. Children need to feel that they can be empowered and that bullying should not be a regular part of their life.

The first week Jeremy sat in my office, he truly believed that he should just accept being bullied as part of his daily school life. Over the course of 10 weeks, though, Jeremy, his parents, and I worked on skill-building activities, which we will talk about in-depth in this book, such as learning to use positive self-talk, as well as effective role playing techniques. I began discussions with his family on how to help their son better address bullying, and on how to better address bullying themselves. We discussed the framework of the Three Es, which stands for empathy, empowerment, and engagement.

Jeremy and his parents worked in sessions and role plays on how to use empathy, empowerment, and engagement to help Jeremy address bullying issues when they took place at school. Jeremy's parents learned methods of starting conversations that allowed productive dialogue, based on empathy and an understanding, of their child's belief that nothing would ever get better. His parents voiced their frustrations with not knowing how to help their child feel better about being bullied daily and worked on methods to empower Jeremy, and to work on finding solutions. And together, we engaged the school and other resources to carry out a plan to help Jeremy cope with the bullying situation.

Jeremy's father told me after just one week of implementing these new techniques, he already felt more aware of how he should approach topics with his son on the issue of bullying, and found a new awareness that was not previously there. Jeremy's father felt more empowered with his newfound understanding of how to handle bullying and how to talk to his son about it.

I wonder, if during that very first session together (or even before they'd come to my office), had Jeremy's father known to react with more empathy and self-regulation to his son's situation, would Jeremy have reacted differently? Jeremy may not have been in tears by the end of the session. If his parents had been able to show more empathy and hear their son's pain, Jeremy may have ended up feeling better.

This is not a critique of my client and his parents, but rather serves to demonstrate that when you have a clearer understanding of your own emotions, you can feel powerful instead of powerless. If you have control over your own emotions and learn to self-regulate more, you can better address crisis points when they happen.

You have your own fears and worries, as of course you want your children to thrive. And as a therapist, I wouldn't suggest that you should perfectly regulate your emotions in front of your children. No therapist could coach you through every hypothetical situation on how to react perfectly. Your reaction doesn't always have to be calm, and you don't have to perfectly plan what you're going to say to your child in every given situation, but you should realize that your reaction will determine your child's ability to respond to the bullying.

Our collective goal is to open the space for more dialogue and a better understanding of your child's situation and wounding.

And this is exactly why I'm writing this book. I will give you the tools in this book to begin to improve how you communicate with your child so that you can have conversations that open the doorway for both of you to cope with a bullying situation. Let's talk about an effective framework for approaching your child about the bullying situation, so that your child feels fully supported by you. The framework I recommend you use in your conversations is called the "Three Es."

The Three Es: Empathy, Empowerment, Engagement

The Three Es are **empathy**, **empowerment**, and **engagement**, and you'll be hearing a lot about them in this book. They are the tools that will help you take your child from being hopeless, to being hopeful. Here you'll find a brief introduction, and in the next chapters, we'll break them down, one-by-one.

In empathy, you learn how to understand your child's feelings and perspective without judgment. It means getting out of your head and into their shoes, and trying your best to feel what she feels. When you use an approach with empathy, you show your child you understand her world and thoughts.

Empathy is not always an easy concept to understand, and may also require practice. In my program, I spend a full session focusing on **role play**, where I have parents practice the idea of true empathy and what it looks like. During role play, the parent will act out a situation, as if she were her child. Simultaneously, the child might act as the counterpart, pretending to be the parent. When two people enter this game-like scenario, playing each other's roles, they can begin to understand why the other might feel a particular way.

Once I start practicing empathy with parents, it is amazing how different their responses become from the beginning to the end of the session. The exercise of practice and guidance can help parents have some awareness of their own behavior when engaging with their child in a more productive manner.

To **empower** someone is to allow their ideas to be important and to communicate this in an effective manner back to that person. To empower your child who has been bullied is to ask how he wants to handle a bullying situation, and get their feedback and thoughts. This allows parents to convey to their children that their thoughts and ideas are important. Parents play an extremely important role in empowering their child. In the chapter on Empowerment, we'll learn about specific things you can do to create an empowering action plan with your child.

Engagement is the follow through of the plan and refers to you checking in consistently with both your child, as she copes with the bullying, and with any adults or school personnel who have said they would help your child with her bullying situation. The consistent follow through will help your child know she needs to be accountable, and that you as the parent want to help your child solve this problem with a thoughtful plan of action behind the scenes. In the engagement chapter, we'll discuss how the different actors—child, adult, and school—can work together to ensure your child is adequately supported.

Parents get very busy in their own lives with jobs, other children, and their own activities. It is not always an easy task to follow the Three Es approach, but empathy, empowerment, and engagement can really increase your child's self-esteem. The Three Es can help decrease negative thoughts your child may be having, and move your child from feeling hopeless, to hopeful.

Along with our discussion of the Three Es, we will also look into powerful healing tools to help you be your best for your child, including self-care. I'll be continuing my own bullying story throughout the book so you can understand the perspective of a bullied child. If you were bullied, were yourself a bully, or were a bystander, I invite you to join me in the healing power of story, and write down your own childhood experiences.

My mother always wanted me to handle my own problems. She would guide me from the side, and I'm sure she worried about my well-being, and wondered how much longer I would continue to be bullied by these girls.

I remember that summer between fourth grade and fifth grade being particularly hard. Summer was a break from the day-to-day teasing, but I was still anxious and worried about what would happen to me when I returned to school after losing so many friends.

What my 10-year-old self really needed in that moment was the chance to be heard, a place to voice my anxiety and worries without judgement. If I'd had a program like the one I've created as an adult, and if I'd had an understanding of the Three Es, I know I would not have felt so alone in my own pain.

In the next chapters, we'll break down each of the Three Es (Empathy, Empowerment, and Engagement) so that your family can grow together through your child's bullying situation.

And it all begins with empathy.

Chapter 2:
What Is Empathy?

Some people find empathy easy, like my dear friend Whitney.

Whitney has a five-year-old daughter named Simone. Simone is beautiful, strong-willed, and has an amazing sense of self. I have seen my friend Whitney, over time, speak to Simone with kindness, love, gentleness, and understanding of her needs. My friend takes the time to really understand Simone's perspective.

When I am around Whitney and her daughter Simone, I am in complete awe of how easy she makes empathy look. My friend understands the innate need and desire to be present for her daughter and to understand Simone's perspective and feelings. When my friend speaks to Simone, it is always with respect and compassion. This is not to say my friend never gets angry or frustrated with her child, but that she mirrors for her daughter a level of understanding of who she is. Whitney wants to help Simone get all her needs met even when Simone is angry and upset. Whitney never forgets that, even faced with Simone's anguish, figuring out how to understand her daughter is the most important goal.

For example, one evening Whitney told Simone that she had five minutes left to watch her show. Whitney followed up five minutes later and asked Simone to give her the iPad. When Simone ignored her mother's wishes, Whitney went over and gently took the iPad from Simone and reminded her that she had been given a five-minute warning. Simone had started to grow frustrated with her mother's five-minute warning, and now, with Whitney's follow through, her cries escalated with her feelings of frustration to all-out sobbing. Whitney gently went over to Simone and mirrored back to Simone what she thought her daughter was feeling by saying, "I am wondering right now if you are feeling frustrated and angry with Mommy because she told you it was time to put the iPad away?" Whitney made eye contact with Simone and spoke in a gentle but clear voice. Simone continued to cry, but Whitney was right there to process and comfort her daughter's needs.

When I ask Whitney about her own level of frustration as a parent, she says that she does have her moments, but her goal of trying to understand Simone and help her process her needs always takes precedence, even during her angriest and most frustrating times.

How Whitney responds and acts towards Simone is true empathy.

But for many of us, empathy is a challenge. That's why we need to break it down so we can really understand what the word means.

Two steps to empathy

Empathy means understanding another person's perspective from their viewpoint. This can be conveyed by making mirroring statements, as Whitney did when Simone was angry and acting out, when she was given a limit at bedtime. **Mirroring** is simply making a statement that reflects back what the other person is saying or feeling. True empathy combines listening and mirroring.

The first step to empathy: listening to your child's feelings without judgment.

The idea of empathy can be confusing if it is not modeled and taught. In fact, some parents have told me that they felt they were being empathic by telling their children how they feel in a frustrated tone. Saying, "I know you're upset, but that's just the way it's going to be" is not empathic. Saying, "I am wondering if you're feeling upset because I asked you to clean up?" is empathic, especially if you then allow space for your child to freely communicate what she's feeling.

The parents of one of my client's, Lauren, wanted her to come to them more often to talk about the relational bullying she was enduring at school. They told her, "We know you're upset, but we need you to tell us when the girls at school are mean to you."

In this instance, Lauren's parents missed the point: they were imposing an interpretation on Lauren, rather than letting her interpret events in her own life. Instead of telling Lauren how she felt and what she needed to do, they could have approached her in a questioning tone, to ask how she felt, wanting to understand why she did not tell her mother about the relational bullying.

They could have asked, listening and mirroring Lauren's feelings back to her, instead of using an angry or frustrated tone to tell Lauren how she felt.

Empathy is not an easy skill to master, but it can be done. The idea of understanding from another person's perspective is not always easy to do. All human beings come with their own ideas of the world and how they and others should fit into those ideas. If your own working theory or ideas get challenged, it can bring discomfort. It is hard to know how to rectify this, particularly if this feeling is stirred up while you are with your children. The unknown territory of how to relate can be uncomfortable, but I encourage you to hang in and use empathy to talk with your children about bullying, despite any discomfort.

Parents who have had similar experiences as their children can use their own understanding to discuss the bullying that their children are experiencing. If a parent has been bullied and is in touch with how this makes her feel, this is the first step to developing an understanding of her child's experience around being bullied.

It might be hard to understand your child if your experiences of bullying are different, but asking yourself, "What does my child need from me to understand better?" will help you to find some connection with your child's feelings. If you are able to dig deep into your own experience, with the desire to connect with your own child, that will help.

If you were not bullied as a child, it is important that you ask yourself, "How would I feel if what my child is going through had happened to me?" Going a step further would be to say, "If I were in my child's shoes, knowing who he is and how he acts, how would I be feeling right now?" Asking these questions to see how your child truly feels, will allow you to gain a better understanding of your child's perspective, and this is the first step to being empathic.

The second step to empathy: mirroring your child's feelings.

After you have listened to your child's feelings, without expressing any judgement, the second step is to ask yourself, "How can I verbally reflect or mirror to her what my child may be feeling?"

I like to use the words "I wonder" quite a bit, because it is an open-ended way to find out if the emotion you think your child is experiencing is correct. An example of open-ended dialogue that you can use is, "I wonder if you are disappointed in the girls who are calling you names, given they used to be your friends."

Closed dialogue would be saying in a frustrated tone, "You must be feeling angry since these girls were supposed to be your friend. I would be pissed if I were you." This is a way to shut dialogue down with your child. Although what you are saying may be true, this does not leave room for your child to tell you how she feels.

As silly as this may sound, practicing asking how your child may be feeling, in front of a mirror or with someone else, may make the actual delivery easier. Try this simple exercise now. Go stand in front of a mirror, and say, "I'm wondering if you're feeling sad because of something that happened at school today?"

Listen to your own tone of voice. Is your tone gentle or impatient? Watch your eyebrows. Are they raised up, like you're asking a genuine question? Or are they pulled down, like you're angry?

Practice asking open-ended questions in the mirror like this until you feel the way you're asking is gentle, patient, and leaves room for your child to express how he is feeling.

It's true that empathy takes a bit more finesse than just mirroring, so as you become more comfortable with these open-ended questions, you'll find yourself fine tuning how you're asking the question, your tone of voice, your facial expression, and your hand gestures.

Let your child feel

When you begin to ask your child empathic questions, you might notice that your child begins to show signs of stress, and that's okay. All children will experience stress differently. Your child might feel stress very emotionally, which you'll notice in his quick temper or irritability or quietness. Or your child might feel stress in her body. Her neck and face might suddenly turn red and heat up. You might see her actually breathing more quickly or running out of breath more than usual.

Part of empathy is allowing someone else to feel the way that comes naturally. Your child may not respond to stress or the environment the same way you do. Children who are highly sensitive to stimuli may become very stressed around loud noise, bright lights, or too many people. Other children thrive on stimuli and friends.

Take a quiet moment with your child, simply to ask him what he's feeling or what she's thinking about. I'll give you suggestions on how to ask your child in an open-ended way that makes room for an honest conversation, but, for now, remember that if your child is being bullied, he is likely experiencing stress and anxiety, and the intensity of his feelings may be completely new for him.

Open up the space for conversation

One important suggestion I have for parents is not to approach your children in your attempt to be empathic right after you've had a frustrating day. When you're stressed, you are not in the emotional space necessary to really understand your child.

Children need to feel comfortable to engage. I am always very light when I meet with child clients. I have a friendly smile on my face, and my body language and tone shows that I am looking forward to getting to know them. I show, in things that I say, that I really do care and want to build a therapeutic relationship with them. I ask my clients about their hobbies, what they've been watching on TV, what they're looking forward to next. If our conversations were solely focused on bullying, our relationship could begin to feel heavy. By talking about other, more enjoyable things, too, we bring lightness and friendliness to our conversation.

In a similar way, you want your conversations to begin when you are in a good emotional space If you are overwhelmed with your own issues of the moment, coming off a bad day, or more emotional than you normally would be, you might wait to ask your child questions until you've centered yourself.

You don't have to be a blank slate, but do have some awareness of your own emotional space when discussing bullying with your child. Bullying is already a loaded topic. It is helpful to make sure that you are calm when you talk to your child about it. The more present a parent can be with his child around bullying, and not focused on other immediate stressors, the more the conversation will be beneficial for his kids.

Life is hard, and we all face daily struggles and stressors. It is not realistic to expect any one person to always be emotionally present with her kids. However, the time you choose to talk to your child about a loaded topic, such as being bullied, will require more ability and commitment from you to be present and actively engaged in a discussion with your child. If there is any frustration or anger, your child may shut down or fear he is burdening you. It is important when you discuss bullying that you have self-awareness around your thoughts and feelings. This also includes your tone of voice and your body language. You can lose your kids if you approach them in a defensive or frustrated manner, and the opportunity for understanding them will be lost.

Having a dialogue with your child about her feelings is not an easy thing to do, particularly if you didn't have the good luck of having model parents who showed you how to be empathic. If you do not usually have close conversations with your child, you should not shy away from trying. It is important even if you are a person who does not talk about your feelings or how others feel very often, that you try the process of thinking about your own experiences and then simply asking: "How are you feeling, right now?" Empathy ultimately brings a family closer together.

Remember that because your child may not want to intentionally burden or anger you, he may want to try and handle his own emotions and feelings. If you are unable to manage your emotions, or if your child sees that you are visibly upset by the bullying, he may shut down in fear of burdening you further with his issues. It's equally unproductive, though, if you are unable to show any emotional connection to your child's experience because he may think you don't care at all.

Parents struggle with empathy for various reasons besides their own frustrations or triggers. This includes how they, themselves, were parented. If they felt the way *their* parents raised them was effective, they may feel the same approach will work well with their own children. On the other hand, parents may have had poor parenting experiences themselves, and may want to respond differently with their own children, still not understanding their own childhood wounds and how this can affect their decisions.

Parents may react with defensiveness when they cannot or will not be able to understand their children. Parents can try to justify their actions and come up with reasons for why their child's perspective does not make sense. Children may respond with shutting down if they do not feel heard.

For example, Lauren got very upset by her parents' reaction when they found out about her relational bullying. She shut down in the session. The cycle becomes very frustrating for both the child and the parent in terms of the expectation each has with the other. Parents and their children will both feel more frustrated if they cannot communicate effectively with each other.

If we don't open up the space for empathy, we miss the opportunity to understand how someone else is feeling. In the session that was supposed to be a celebration for Lauren and her parents, working through Lauren's bullying situation together, lack of empathy led instead to more anger and frustration by the end of the session. Lauren's parents had a hard time understanding and processing her perspective. Unknowingly, they were not able to show true empathy in a manner that left Lauren feeling safe. Instead, the session ended with tears and worry that her parents were angry with her.

Lauren's parents could have made some attempts at empathy by asking more open-ended questions in the session. Instead of saying, "Things will never change," "We've been dealing with this problem for *so long*," and "Why are you so sensitive?" in a pleading, impatient tone of voice, her parents could have said, "I am wondering how you are feeling right now?" That would have been a better attempt to be present in the moment for their daughter.

If they would have stopped their reactions to their own triggers and sought out what her experience was in the moment, they could have connected with her and understood her better. This was a perfect opportunity as parents to make an attempt to understand their child's perspective, despite their own feelings of anger and frustration. I am not saying empathy is easy to utilize—indeed, it is a learned skill—but the more a parent is able to make attempts to understand who his or her children are, with all their beauty and limitations, the more he or she will be able to have a helpful and productive conversation.

In practicing empathy, it is important to use questions and statements such as, "I am wondering if you feel sad today?" Ask questions and practice this skill with others. Come up with a scenario and play it through to help with the practice of empathy. Empathy is a complex skill to learn. I think once this skill is practiced more frequently, with time, it can lead to a greater understanding of your child. I know you want to be responsive to your child and to learn the best ways to talk to your child. It is just not always easy to leave your own emotions out of the process.

Let's take you through an example. Jane comes into my office her with her 10-year-old son, Sam. Sam had an unusually bad day with kids teasing him at school. In this session, Jane is practicing the skills of empathy:

Therapist: How is everyone doing today?

Jane: This has been a hard day for Sam. I noticed when he got in the car before coming here that he seemed upset.

Therapist: Were you able to have a dialogue to understand what was bothering Sam? Shall we ask Sam?

Jane: I tried to ask him why he seemed so upset but he shut down.

Sam: I am fine Mom. Stop worrying.

Therapist: Sam, I am wondering if you felt upset at some of the other kids today? Are you worried if you tell your mom what happened that she may worry more about you?

Sam: NO, I am fine. She does not need to worry.

Therapist: I agree that you do not want your mother to worry about you, but as a parent, she will worry knowing that something upset you. Would you feel comfortable sharing what bothered you at school today? Jane, I am wondering if there is a way you can convey to Sam that your biggest concern is that you want Sam to just be honest with you without any judgement for what happened?

Jane: Sam, honey, I just want you to tell me what is bothering you so I have a better idea how to help you. When you feel sad, I feel sad. I do not want you to worry about my feelings. I can take care of myself. I just want to understand you.

Sam: Okay, this is what happened ...

Be open to hearing your child's perspective and feelings, without judgment. Jane was able to convey to Sam that whatever he felt and whatever happened at school, he would not be judged. She just wanted to be there for him and his pain, which she could see, quite visibly, on his face.

There may be times when you struggle to be empathic, but keep trying. With practice, you will become a more empathic parent and the relationship between your child and yourself will be strengthened.

Vulnerability makes true empathy possible

One of the reasons we, as adults, particularly struggle with empathy is because our society teaches us to be strong, that we shouldn't have moments where we feel like life is overwhelming and we just need to cry. Parents also may worry what it would mean to feel emotions and express the understanding of what others think and feel. To be vulnerable is one of the rawest forms of human emotion.

I have shared the most vulnerable parts of who I am with my friend Whitney. She shows me with her words and body language that she can handle and hear my pain. Hearing about pain can be a lot for some people and can make them uncomfortable.

As a parent, you may feel flooded with someone expressing too much emotion. It can overwhelm you, since you may be carrying around many of your own burdens. Parents may have many of their own challenges that they are dealing with, and cannot spare another place emotionally inside themselves to be present for their child and their feelings.

We all have our limits of what we can handle and tolerate, and have our defenses for a reason.

You, as the parent, need to be honest with your limits and how to work within limits or boundaries. It would be unfair and unrealistic to put yourself in a position of overloading yourself emotionally. The end result would not be helpful for you or your child. We need to work within the limits of emotional capacity and be able to help people find value in where they are at. You can work on these limitations by asking questions such as, "What does my child need from me right now to help her feel better? How can I be more present for her with the limitations I have right now?"

Lauren's mother struggled through a few different sessions of being unable to really address her emotions surrounding her *own* bullying. She would speak about the bullying as if it had happened to a distant cousin that she had not had much contact with in years. She would own her bullying, but never shared the experience or emotion behind this feeling. I sat there and listened to Lauren's mother, and I hoped that she could get in touch with some emotion and pain that she felt. In the session, I knew I could not push this parent to a limit of discomfort. I knew if I pushed her at all on the emotions behind being bullied, that she would tense up and I would lose her.

When you are reflecting on your own childhood memories and trying to be empathic for your child, know that you will find your own emotional limits. Be kind and patient with yourself, too, as you try to open yourself up to this vulnerable experience of connecting with your child.

Even if you don't have the experience of bullying, being vulnerable with your child is crucial to opening the space for empathy. One father, Kent, who came to me with his daughter who had been bullied, expressed quite honestly in the session that he was a popular kid and never was bullied. But Kent still asked the questions, "How can I understand my child's experience with bullying, so I can be there for her?" In the session, he could think about his daughter's needs and his own need to really find a way to understand her experience. The desire to understand our children is the first step to being empathic.

I have had parents who do not want to talk about their own emotions, come to me with their children. They want to focus only on their children and on making their children better. I feel that I get put in a bind when parents are clear from the beginning that their own feelings cannot be brought into the therapy room. I feel we miss an opportunity to empathically attune to the parents' emotions, which can in turn help their child feel safer to express herself. Safety is important when emotions are present. I always validate parents around their limits, but I leave room for them to feel safe to express their emotions. When the parents begin to feel safer, I gently suggest that it may be important for their child to see some of the parent's emotions, to bond the child and parent closer. This would mean maybe talking to their child about their own childhood experiences around bullying and how they felt.

In the final graduation session with Lauren and her family, her mother sat half twisted away from everyone on the couch, making little eye contact. When she did finally turn toward everyone else, she looked very frustrated and flooded with her own emotions. I turned to Lauren's mother and wanted to give her a moment to share how she felt, which was obvious in her body language. Unfortunately, at this time, Lauren's mother was not willing to be vulnerable by sharing her own emotions.

But I want more for you and for your child. You'll find that if you can begin an empathic conversation with your child and then be open and vulnerable with your feelings, too, you will establish a new style of conversation. Imagine, you might sit down with your child and start the conversation by saying, "I'm wondering if you're sad because of something that happened at school today." And within a few minutes, you might hear your child mirror back to you, "I'm wondering if you're upset because you care about me?" *That's* the kind of empathic conversation I want to make possible for you and for your child.

Children and empathy

But children are not naturally empathic, either. Kids can hurt each other without even being aware of it at times, simply because they don't always know what is kind and what is unintentionally mean.

I was talking to an adolescent, female client, Renee, who was sharing some of the dialogue she had with her friends. There was a girl at her school, who we'll call Denise. Denise was making mean comments about Renee to Renee's friends. Later that day, Renee's friends, thinking they were being loyal, good friends, repeated back the negative comments made about her. Renee was shocked that Denise had so much dislike towards her. It left Renee feeling vulnerable and hurt that these comments were made about her.

Renee and I then talked about empathy and how other people can identify with someone's feelings. Initially, she felt her friends were being loyal for wanting her to know this. When I asked if the information she now had was helpful and had meaning to her, she realized that although not done with ill intentions, it hurt her feelings and made her more uncomfortable around Denise. She realized in this moment that her friends were not demonstrating true empathy or understanding by telling her something that left her feeling more vulnerable. This is an example of blocking an empathic discussion. Renee's friends could not see that telling her these mean comments would hurt Renee. Rather, they thought that by telling her, they were doing the right thing.

Renee's friends did not mean to be hurtful to her, but there was a clear lack of understanding of Renee's perspective—how she would feel hearing these comments and whether it would be more hurtful to share this information with her.

Children block empathic discussions when they do not understand what it means to have empathy. For children to learn empathy, they need parents and other adults to model this skill to them. Start with asking a question, such as, "I was wondering, what do you think?" If Renee's friends had chosen not to say anything to her and thought about how these comments would affect Renee negatively, that would have been empathic in this situation. But if there had been dialogue after the hurtful information had been shared; that is, if her friends had come to her and apologized for telling her the mean comments, this would also be showing empathy on their part.

The issue of how hurtful Renee's friends were being came out of another conversation in my office where Renee was bringing up her friends. But I thought this was a perfect opportunity to take her through the whole scenario and then ask her if her friends telling her these specific, mean comments really made her feel better.

Therapist: I think it would be important, Renee, to role play one of the situations with your friends. It may be helpful to have a better understanding of what is happening for you.

Renee: Okay, I guess.

Therapist: Renee, can you give me a recent example of a time that this group of girls said or did something cruel to you?

Renee: Well, yesterday at school I was sitting in class, and I heard a few of them behind me start to laugh and seemed to use a code word that I did not know. But every time I spoke up in class, they started to laugh and use this code name.

Therapist: How did this make you feel when they would laugh at you?

Renee: It embarrassed me, but whatever.

Therapist: I am wondering if you were embarrassed and might be trying to push down any feelings you may have had about the situation? Is this maybe true?

Renee: I guess, but it would not help to get more upset. There is nothing I can do about this.

Therapist: Yes, you cannot control their behavior and actions, but you do have control over your reactions and responses in this situation.

Renee: What do you mean?

Therapist: How did you respond to the girls when they started to laugh?

Renee: I got really sad and put my head down.

Therapist: I am wondering if you felt so tired by this point and felt there was nothing you could truly do to defend yourself?

Renee: Yeah, there is nothing I can do. They keep doing this.

Therapist: I understand the feelings you may have, but you have more power than you think. You still can control your reactions to situations and your own feelings—they do not have power over you.

Renee: I guess.

Therapist: What do you think you could do differently next time? Let's role play the situation, and I want you to now think about how you could change your tone of voice to show that you are in control of yourself and your actions. I know this is hard.

Renee: Okay, I will have you play the girls and tell you some of their mean comments and I will show a difference in my own reactions.

Therapist: Sounds good. Let's try this a few times with no reaction and what you would do differently.

When I was taking Renee through this scenario, it was as if a light clicked and she realized that her friends were not really making her feel better by giving her this information. As a parent, you may find yourself in a position, where you feel the need to show your child that kids sometimes are hurtful to their peers by relaying to her things other kids are saying. Kids often have no awareness of how sharing this gossip affects the friend who is being talked about, but you can model the conversation I had with Renee in your own home, to help your child see that it's actually hurtful to know the gossip.

I think back to my time in the fourth grade when I was ditched by a group of girls, and I told my mother at home how sad and worried I was about how I would handle the next day at school.

My mother felt that she did not have the education and understanding for what bullying was when I was a child. She did the best she could with limited awareness of how to help me. I was all alone with my pain and sadness. My mother could not help take the pain away from me, even as much as she tried to. I remembered feeling very hurt and wounded by these girls, almost as if it was yesterday.

I wonder if this feeling of not knowing what to do or having a lack of awareness is similar for many parents, besides my own mother.

What a gift you can give to your child, to simply listen and mirror with compassion.

Chapter 3:
Empowerment

———➤◄———

Empowerment means helping your child have the confidence he needs to make his voice heard. This does not mean speaking for your child. If you take over and don't allow your child to talk, or if you configure his thoughts and ideas, this is not empowering him. Rather, encourage your child to share his own thoughts and opinions. Let me clarify with an example.

As a therapist who works closely with children and families who are learning to cope with bullying, I often accompany my parents to school meetings to educate and support both the parent and the school on working together to address the bullying. The other day, I accompanied my client, Danny and his father to a first meeting with the school. Danny is currently being physically and verbally bullied by some of the other kids at school, particularly during physical education class. The other kids will push him and threaten him and get up in his face. Danny's father has had a few previous conversations with the school principal, regarding Danny's bullying. His father felt the meeting with the principal was effective, as the principal conveyed that she heard their concerns, yet the bullying continued. However, Danny felt his voice was getting lost.

Before the meeting began, I sat with Danny and his father to talk about the questions that I would ask in the meeting. I encouraged and empowered Danny to speak his concerns and let the adults in the room know how it felt to not be heard.

In the meeting, we addressed Danny's bullying and how he felt. We went through all the recent physical bullying that had taken place and allowed Danny to assert himself, explaining how he'd tried to handle the situation.

I validated Danny many times in the school meeting for having the courage to address the principal and vice principal, allowing them to see his vulnerabilities. Danny's father also empowered Danny before the school meeting by encouraging him to speak up and allow his voice to be heard, as well as in helping Danny figure out how to best share his concerns. During the meeting itself, Danny's father continued to say aloud that he felt what Danny was saying had value and his words were important to be heard.

When the meeting ended, Danny and his father had huge smiles on their faces. They felt, for the first time, that Danny was being listened to and heard. Danny's father had a sense of relief that his child's needs were not only being expressed, but also being heard. Danny's voice was important and had an impact on the outcome of the situation. It was clear how much Danny valued communication and how critical it was that his feelings were being validated.

After Danny had this corrective experience with feeling empowered for the first time in a very long time, he no longer had people incorrectly assume how he felt and was no longer being told to figure things out himself. Rather, there were people who took his ideas and feelings in, really listened to him, and assured him that they would address the bullying.

Speak your truth and be heard

Children often feel disempowered, that their voice is not important, and is overlooked or ignored when they are being bullied. It is important when we empower children, to show encouragement and also to follow through in implementing their ideas, to show them that their thoughts are important.

You empower your child by allowing your child's voice to be heard. As an example of an empowering statement would be a parent saying, "Son, I think you have some great feedback to add to the meeting today, and it is important for the principal and the vice principal to hear your thoughts and words. I will be there to support you." This statement is empowering your child to make his voice heard.

But listening is not enough. In this chapter, I will challenge you to work with your child to come up with a **bullying action plan** that details how she wants to handle the bullying. I'll provide a template for you to use to create your own bullying action plan, but the larger idea, here, is to show your child with your words and support that you trust her ideas and actions, and will support and stand by her, as Shawn did with his son Danny.

Often parents think they need to speak for their kids, perhaps because they have felt that other adults have not listened to their kids. It is understandable that parents feel that they need to step in when the adults around them have not taken care of the problem because parents do not want to see their kids suffer.

But the idea of empowerment with bullying is for you to ask your child to develop a bullying action plan and to have your child take you through the plan, while you support her ideas and provide guidance along the way. Let her know that what she has to say matters.

If Danny's father had taken over the meeting and spoken for his son, explaining what his son felt, no matter how good his intentions, Danny would not have been empowered. It's true that there are times, if kids do not want to actually speak in the meeting, that the adult can speak on their behalf. But in the case with Danny's father, he checked in with what his son felt comfortable with and decided that if he had spoken for Danny, it would not have been empowering for his son.

When you seek to empower your child, you are saying to her that her voice needs to be heard and that others cannot speak on her behalf as well as she can. In two simple empowerment steps, first, allow your child to speak, and, second, encourage your child to come up with her own plan to address the bullying.

Empowerment is not just telling your child to "handle it"

Empowering your child to come up with a bullying action plan to handle his bullying situation is not the same as telling him to "handle it" on his own. Some parents believe the only way to get bullying to stop is for the child to stand up for himself. But that places unfair pressure on a child to resolve a problem which is much larger than just one relationship between a bully and victim.

One of my clients, Adam, faced this situation of being expected to "handle" his own bully. Adam played on a baseball team. His father witnessed the other kids bullying Adam during baseball practice, calling his son names and taunting him. Adam's father shared many times that he felt frustrated and helpless, watching his son break down in tears after he tried to advocate for himself with the coach, many times on his own. Adam's father wanted the bullying to stop and felt that the verbal bullying was now turning to physical bullying, as his son was regularly coming home with bruises. Adam's father had attempted on many occasions to discuss with Adam how he could better confront the other kids on the baseball team, but the kids continued to bother him, and the coaches were not responsive to helping to stop the bullying.

Once the kids were not only taunting Adam, but starting to leave more and more bruises, Adam's father decided it was time for him to talk to the coach. I encouraged the father to talk through what the discussion with the coach should be. Although it came to a point where his son's safety was a concern, it was still important for Adam's father to be part of the plan of action to make sure Adam's voice was heard. It was also important to check in with Adam to make sure if the kids continued any of their bullying, that Adam still felt safe and comfortable going back to his father.

Adam was worried at first that his father was going to stop him from being heard, but instead his father made Adam feel important by asking for Adam's input on how he should approach the coach. His father, Jack, also suggested that Adam come and talk to the coach with him, so that Adam's voice *could* be heard. Now, Adam's father knows to speak to the coach without disempowering his son or taking over the process of finding a solution because he sees the importance of involving his son's opinions and ideas.

Empowerment is encouraging your child to lead with your guidance. Letting your child handle her bullying issues totally by herself, giving her no guidance, and leaving her completely alone to carry out her own action plans, without offering any follow through, is certainly not empowering. When you empower your child, you let her know you are by her side to guide her, not by providing all the answers, but by helping her come up with her own conclusions.

Nor is empowerment allowing your child to express any feeling he has, in any way he feels (hitting younger siblings or yelling at parents, for example). Empowerment is not giving your child free rein. You may fear that if you empower your child, you will lose control, but true empowerment is about responsibility, and you have to start giving your child responsibility as he matures. Empowering your child gives him space to mature, and because you'll remain engaged with your child, you'll still be available as a guide.

It is important that you do not try to always be the voice for your kids. You want to protect your child and may be worried about the outcome if you do not step in. However, if you can empower your child to solve his own conflicts, you can still be in the driver's seat while your child has his hand on the wheel. This essentially means that your child needs guidance from you, but does not need you telling him what to say and do. If you can learn how to empower, you can help your child by guiding him without taking over.

Empowerment can really work to ameliorate bullying, as you can see with Danny and his father, Shawn, in the following example:

> *Shawn: So, Danny, we have a school meeting coming up with your principal and vice principal. I am wondering how you feel about this, and I am wondering if you would like to participate?*
>
> *Danny: I don't really know. The vice principal doesn't listen to me when I go to him. What difference does it make if I attend this meeting? It won't change things.*
>
> *Shawn: Am I right to say you sound frustrated right now with the situation? If this is the case, it is even more important for the adults to hear what you feel. I care very much that the adults hear what you have to say. It will bring more weight coming from you rather than me or your therapist. I am willing to sit here and talk through what you want to say to them before we go to the meeting, and practice to help you feel more comfortable, but I really do feel your voice is the most important one. But I will support the decision you make.*
>
> *Danny: I'm not sure what to say.*
>
> *Shawn: Well let's start with what attempts you've made to stop the bullying. What do you think about giving specific examples to the principal and vice principal? How would this sound?*
>
> *Danny: So, I tell them that I told the kids to stop and I walked away and they still followed me?*
>
> *Shawn: Yes. That is perfect. Give them specific examples when this happened and how you tried to handle the*

bullying yourself I know you also mentioned another issue. Was it that the adults that you spoke to were not listening to you and told you to handle the problem yourself? If so, how would you feel bringing this to their attention, as well? Danny: All I can say is that I went to the coach at PE, and he told me to handle the problem myself. That was it.

Shawn: My suggestion is you do just that. How would that feel to you? Would this be something you're comfortable with?

Danny: Yes, I could do that.

Shawn: Okay. It sounds like we have a plan. Do you want to review it or do you feel that you are ready for tomorrow? Remember I will be there to support you the entire way

Danny: I'm good. Thanks, Dad!

In this example, Shawn took his son from a hopeless place to a hopeful one just by guiding the conversation with suggestions, but allowing his son to decide what he wanted to say. This is an exact example of a parent taking their child through the steps of empowerment. Danny felt further empowered by his father, instead of disempowered, because of the manner in which he asked his son questions and showed that his responses mattered. Danny felt his voice was important and what he said did matter.

After the school meeting, Shawn knew that follow-up would be required. He needed to continue to make sure that his son felt confident about his voice being heard. He did not want to see his son re-victimized for speaking up against the bully to the adults at school. This is a real fear that kids have when they speak up, the fear that the peers who bullied them will retaliate and re-victimize them. That is why checking back in and making sure the bullying has been addressed is important.

Asking for help requires strength

Remind your kids that although it's not easy, when they use their voice, people will listen. Empowerment is not a one-time skill, but one that is continued to be built upon, over and over again, as more challenges or experiences are faced by your child. Teach your child that asking for help shows strength and character.

Earlier, we discussed the case of Adam, who was being bullied on the baseball field. Adam had tried many times to solve the bullying and used many different skills, and his father empowered Adam the whole way through. However, it got to a point that safety was an issue. Adam was getting hurt and bruised by the other kids who would not stop. It is always important to consider your child's safety. If you truly feel a pattern of continued abuse is happening, it might be time to have the adults intervene. In the situation with Adam, we still empowered him as much as we could until the situation got dangerous. We wanted Adam to handle the situation by going back to the kids and trying his own plan first, before the adults intervened. When his father did intervene, he still wanted Adam to be part of the process.

Some children will naturally need more parental guidance than others. Ask your child for her action plan, but also use your own judgement to think about whether there is a clear action plan that is detail-oriented and seems to really make sense for your child. Or, is your child saying, "I don't know" frequently? It is important to first ask your child what she is thinking her action plan will be, then judge how much guidance your child needs, depending on her age, level of maturity, personality, ability to problem solve, and the situation.

If your child is very depressed and feels hopeless, it may take more encouragement and guidance than it would for a child who is good at problem solving and likes to participate in a solution. Bullying can bring all sorts of emotions out, and there is never one easy answer.

Bullying triggers many different emotions in all those who are affected by it, at all levels. Your child may be feeling hurt, alone, and powerless. You may be brought back to your own childhood by emotions triggered from being bullied. You may also feel angry and frustrated that your child is being bullied. You may want your kid to fight back so the bully knows your child is not weak, with the hope the bully will never strike your child again.

It is not easy for you to hear your child is being bullied. You are watching the effects of the bullying with your child in front of him. You do not like to see your children in pain or suffering. You want to take your children's pain away as my mother wished she had many years ago. The feeling of seeing your child suffer is very hard for parents. You want to make the bullying go away so your child will no longer suffer.

But know that your child may be stronger than you think. Give your child space to grow and mature. His maturity level will change over time when you see how he has handled previous situations. For example, Shawn knew Danny could handle being in the school meeting and sharing his feelings. He knew that Danny had the strength to tolerate being in front of other adults and felt his father supported him.

There are other kids who may not be as strong, and who many feel disempowered. Those children may need more support, guidance, and help coming up with an action plan. You may need to intervene and instead of asking your child how she wants to handle the problem, you may need to provide actual suggestions. But even in the process of offering suggestions, you can still encourage your child to decide which plan would work best. You can also make sure her ideas are used to come up with the plan. This is consistent with reminding your child that her voice and ideas are important.

Before you can begin to address bullying, you must remember to be empathic and seek to understand your child's perspective. You, as the parent, cannot move to the next step without understanding where your child is at emotionally, and getting an understanding of the bullying situation. You cannot go right away into action or empowerment mode without having a clear understanding of the problem and how your child feels. However, empathy alone is not enough to help your child address the bullying. It will help if you understand the emotional state of your child, but you still need the guidance of a plan. Reflect on what you think your child is feeling, then ask her for ideas of how she wants to handle the situation.

Empathy and empowerment are a powerful combination for kids to feel heard, and to feel that there is hope to change their current situation, and most importantly, for kids to feel that their parent will be there to support them. The flow of empathy starts with open-ended questions which lead to empowerment, which includes suggestions made by you, of how your child wants to handle the situation at hand, and allowing your child's voice to be heard.

Three steps to empower your child

To empower a child or adolescent requires dialogue that is specific to allowing their voice to be heard, and I'd like to give you some examples to help you empower your child.

Before you start any conversation with your child, make sure you're not preoccupied with other issues. If you do not feel like you have time to sit and discuss a clear plan of action, do not even start. The timing chosen to talk should be good for both of you, a time when you are both in the proper emotional space, so that you will be less distracted and more successful in coming up with a plan.

The foundation to empowerment is always empathy.

Empathy must come before empowerment. As before, listen without judgement and mirror your child's feelings. You can segue to this part of the conversation by asking, "I was wondering how you feel about the cyberbullying?"

The first step to empowerment: ask your child about a plan to handle future bullying.

After your child answers, you listen, and you mirror, you can segue to empowering her by asking, "How do you want to handle the situation next time?" It's important to pose this question to address her thoughts about a plan of action. To truly empower your child, you allow her the room to come up with her thoughts on a bullying action plan. Here's a sample of how this could sound, coming from you:

"I know you have been left out of many activities and are being teased by people who were supposed to be your friends at school. You seem to be coming home depressed. It is hard to see you so upset. I would like to help you through this hard time of being relationally bullied by your friends. What do you feel would be a good way to handle the teasing and other mean behavior? It is important to me that we come up with a clear plan of action. I trust that you have some ideas and want to handle this, but it is important to me that we discuss this. I do trust you and want your voice to be heard and taken seriously. How do you think your voice can be heard? What would this look like?"

This is an example of an empowering dialogue with a child. It is important to let your child know her voice is important and needs to be heard, and that you support her and are not just allowing the bullying to continue.

And you want to continue the empowerment conversation, to make sure your child's bullying action plan is thought-out. You could continue, saying:

"So, the girls who are cyberbullying you are at school. How will you approach them at school? What will you do differently with your social media accounts to change your reaction to them?"

This is asking more specific questions about the plan and finding out how detail-oriented your child can be with the plan of action.

I'd like to provide you with a template for a **bullying action plan**, which is the detailed action-steps that your child will take before, during, and after a bullying incident.

You and your child should talk through the following together:
- When a future incident of bullying is likely to occur
- Where the bullying is likely to occur
- The names of the people who will likely be involved
- What your child should do to avoid the bullying, entirely
- If the bullying does happen, what might be said or done to your child
- What your child should say or do in direct response to the bully
- Which individuals or adults your child should approach afterward
- What your child should say to those adults
- What your child should say to *you* and when the two of you should have a follow-up conversation
- What circumstances will warrant intervention from other adults, school personnel, or authorities

Important note: Your child may say that she can handle things herself and does not want you as the parent to intervene. Here is a sample dialogue I would reply with to this statement.

"I hear how you feel and that you are asking me to trust that you can come up with a plan of action. However, I am worried about you and, as your parent, I would like for you to take me through each step that you plan to take so that I can make sure you're taking care of yourself."

It can be a reflective statement back, but it makes clear that a plan of action will need to be discussed with you.

Now, with you and your child on the same page, you can practice the plan, together.

The second step to empower your child: role play the plan.

Remember when I encouraged you and your child to role play so that you could increase empathy for each other's perspectives? Here, with empowerment, you can use role play again. You may ask, *"How would you feel if we role play how you will respond and I play one of the other kids, so we can practice the plan together?"*

This allows the practicing of a role play to give your child a sense of feeling in control of the situation. You can also have her take you through a typical scenario of how she thinks this will play out.

The third step to empower your child: check in with how your child is feeling about this plan.

Start with a simple, "I wonder" question, and give your child space to say what she's thinking and feeling. Together, you can make any fine-tuning or changes based on the situation, and you can practice any other action plans.

As you wrap up this empowering conversation with your child, remind her that you will be following up to see how this plan went. This way, your child knows that you are involved and want to have oversight over how things are going.

Different temperaments require different approaches

Different children react differently to bullying, which means we must adapt the way we empower them according to their type.

The first is an *easily-angered child*. Kids who are easily prone to angry outbursts may require a review in anger management skills. You can take your child through how to relax and use anger management skills, such as deep breaths, asking for help from an adult, or walking away from a situation that causes anxiety. It is also important, if your child is being bullied and has a short temper, that *you* practice helpful coping skills to address feelings of anger that may arise in you, as well. Role playing potential scenarios would also be helpful for both you and your child.

Let's take an example:

"I am wondering if the cyberbullying is making you really angry and you want to respond aggressively to your peers? I can understand how you feel, but let's discuss some ways to help you calm down in the moment with your anger, and find more productive ways to handle the cyberbullying where they cannot make you any angrier. I know you can do this, and believe what you think is important and needs to be heard. How does it sound if we start with some scenarios that may make you angry and then we practice ways to handle your anger? Then, we can discuss some suggestions specific to how to help you address the cyberbullying. Does this sound good?"

This is an example of speaking to a child who is prone to anger. As you can see, this child may need some initial coaching and support from the parent on how to calm his anger down. Until he is calmed down, he will not be able to have a good plan of action without retriggering the child. The parent explains that he will help his child breathe and manage his anger. Role playing to provoke anger and breathing deeply to calm anger will help, before you can implement that clear, detailed action plan together.

If your child is *prone to crying, very sensitive, and easily embarrassed,* it is important that you remember this when approaching her. Have her speak to another adult about how she feels and assess her feelings about her own self-esteem. If your child is sensitive and very depressed, it is important that you provide further guidance and support to make sure she knows she can be helped, such as, "I am wondering if you feel really sad right now? And if so, I am here to help you come up with a plan, and make some helpful suggestions for you to handle the bullying with your peers."

If your child is very sensitive or gets upset easily, it is important to provide the coping skills such as positive self-talk, as well as the ability to find an adult to talk to if she becomes overly flooded with information and needs help to process her feelings before going back to handle the situation with the bully. This may include some work with role plays if your child is open to this.

An example of part of this dialogue may be:

"I am wondering if your feelings were hurt by the other girls leaving you out of the party, especially since one of them was supposed to be your friend? It sounds like they're leaving you out and ignoring you. I am wondering if this is hurting your feelings. Can we discuss ways to handle your sadness when these thoughts arise? I want to help you feel better and practice positive self-talk that you are special, when you get hurt by these girls. Can we do this before putting a plan together to handle the bullying? I want to make sure you are comfortable with the plan and that we address any sadness you may have."

In this example, we use positive self-esteem building skills. An example of positive self-talk here is, "I know I am a good person, even if the other girls are leaving me out." Practice positive self-talk instead of stating that you deserve to be left out or asking why they would leave you out. It is important to replace negative self-talk statements with positive ones, as the example above shows. Then, once you as the parent have addressed her feelings, you can empower your child to come up with a plan of action.

You may also have a *quiet child* who does not give much information about the bullying. If this happens, it is important to ask a lot more detail-oriented questions to get a better sense of what is going on and how to help your child. Here are sample questions you can use in a dialogue:

"I am wondering what kind of bullying you are experiencing? Would you feel comfortable telling me who is bullying you and how these situations are getting started? Can you tell me what these kids are saying or doing to you and how this happens? How often are they bullying you—daily or weekly? Have you thought of some ways you can address this type of bullying with your peers? What are some ideas you have already had? Do you want to review, with my guidance, some ideas of ways to address the bullying with your peers? I can go through some ideas and thoughts based on information you give me. Then, we can figure out how to best hear your voice, because what you have to say is important. Would this be helpful?"

This example gives your child more guidance to answer specific questions, since they are very quiet and harder to engage in giving answers. Parents may need to dig deeper to get more answers to the questions, to help guide and support a quieter, less interested, or less talkative child.

Or you may have an *independent child* who may feel he can handle his issues alone and does not feel there is any value in asking you for help. This child feels he can handle the problem, although you know the bullying has not stopped and is not getting better. Here is an example of dialogue you may use:

"I am wondering if you would rather not be talking through your plan of action with me? I want to check in with what your thoughts are right now. Can you take me through your plan of action to handle the bullying? I have complete confidence in you and just because I want you to take me through the entire plan, does not mean I do not think you cannot handle your plan all by yourself. But I want to make sure that the bullying gets better, and you and I both know it has not. All I want to do is fine-tune and review the plan you feel will work. Let's just make sure there is not anything we are missing. I agree that you're strong and independent. I want to make sure the other kids know not to bother you anymore. Does this make sense to you?"

This independent child needs to be empowered for being independent; remind him that you value his independence and self-reliance. Make sure the child knows his ideas are important, while identifying where he needs to be supported by his parents who know more. Talking through an action plan and scenario, and providing feedback, can help the independent child. This independent child may actually deem the feedback as helpful guidance, not taking away from his own independence around his ideas of how to deal with the bullying.

Re-visiting a disempowering conversation

Now that we've learned the ins and outs of empowerment, let's consider my client Lauren and her mother, who were upset at finding out Lauren's bullying had continued without her letting them know. If this family was able to do a "do-over," how could they utilize both empathy and empowerment guiding each step?

The foundation to empowerment is always empathy.

Lauren's mother: *"I am wondering how you are feeling about the bullying going on? I know I was taken aback that it was still happening. I'm sorry the way I conveyed this to you was not supportive, and I'm sorry I sounded angry. How are you feeling about what happened in the last session? I am wondering if you were upset because you thought I was mad at you after I found out that the bullying was continuing?"* Remember, when being empathic, use open-ended questions to understand how your child is feeling, to learn more about where he is, emotionally.

Then, you can move on to empowerment:

Lauren's mother*: "I realized that I did not give you a good chance to tell me about the bullying and how you want to handle this. I instead made statements to you. I want to know, how do you want to handle the situation so this does not continue? What would you like to do? I will need you to walk through or role play certain scenarios with me so I know how you want to handle this. I just want you to know how much I care about you, and I will be here to help you through this. I trust your ability to handle the bullying with my help and support."*

This is an example of giving empowering statements, and trusting that Lauren can handle the problem by asking her to provide guidance to her mother of how she will address the problem. At no time in the above example was the mother asking Lauren to handle things alone, without her mother being there to support and guide her if necessary. Lauren's mother also showed that she was now aware of how she previously came off and was trying to correct herself by acknowledging this, coming at Lauren in a less aggressive fashion, and one that showed more patience and awareness for her daughter's bullying. It is important that both of these steps are done, within a time frame that allows for the parent to stay present with their child in the moment.

Even if you are able to empathize with your child, please know that your child needs more than just empathy. Your child needs to know that her voice and ideas are important and that she (with your help) can create a bullying action plan to cope with her bullying situation.

I think back to my own emotional needs, as a 10-year-old being bullied. While I knew that my mother felt sad for me, my lack of feeling empowered still left me at the mercy of my bullies.

I remember the summer after I was ditched by the other girls. I remember being at home in my room crying. I was extremely anxious and worried, and very lonely. I did not have friends to play with and my companion was the TV or my babysitter while my parents worked. My parents had not discussed a plan of action with me in the fall for going back to school. I had no idea what was to come. I would have days when I was very distraught and depressed, not knowing what the coming year would bring.

If I'd had someone to talk through a plan about how to address the girls at school, and if she had role played this with me, this may have alleviated some of my anxiety and fears about going back to school for my fifth-grade year. I remembered their mean comments about how I looked and acted. Everything about me, they laughed about. The girls would make fun of any aspect of who I was—my clothes, my body, the way I talked, what I ate for lunch, everything. Their mean statements stayed in my head throughout the entire summer and my worry and anxiety crept forward. The pressure was on for me to go back to the same school where I felt rejected by the entire class, in which I had very few, if any, friends to play with. I would need to summon some courage and strength from somewhere, if I was to go back to school and face the girls who had hurt me and broken my confidence.

Chapter 4:
Engagement

Empathy paves the way for understanding your child. Empowerment reassures your child, that his voice is heard and valued as a part of creating an action plan. Now, it's time for you to **engage** your child in carrying out the plan and making sure further follow through happens. It also involves the way in which someone approaches the plan of action. As an example, let me share with you the story of John.

John was 12 years old, very smart and secure, and he had good self-esteem. He came to the program to address some physical and verbal bullying that he was experiencing during recess every day at school. John discussed ways that he had previously advocated for himself by going to the aides on the yard, talking to a school principal, or having his mother advocate for him with the principal. When John started coming to sessions, he seemed secure in knowing what was right and wrong for how his peers treated him. He felt comfortable telling his mother about some of the bullying that was going on. He even had this attitude of accepting at times that there was some verbal bullying.

But, one day, John became scared. He came to my office for his session and told me he needed some help. I could see in his eyes that something was truly causing him fear and to worry. I started the session by asking how he was feeling. I reflected back to him, that I saw he seemed to have a sad look on his face with some feelings of worry. John told me that he had tried to ignore the other kids and had asked for help from the aide on the yard, but the aide had simply told him to handle things all by himself, even though the other kids were pushing him.

John and his mother had worked hard on addressing the verbal bullying and his feelings. However, John shared that now he was getting pushed on the yard, and when he went to seek help, neither the aides in the yard nor the vice principal at the school made him feel safe. The vice principal's response made John feel that he was on his own, that he would receive no help. He was told to simply handle the problem himself.

The physical bullying was getting worse, and John was starting to feel that even though he was advocating for himself and going to the adults for help, he was not getting the help he needed.

I helped coach John's mother to discuss a plan of action for how John would handle the situation. We discussed ways to avoid these peers and how not to retaliate unless it was for self-defense.

John knew to ignore his peers and *tried* not to give them any attention, even when they'd brush up against him. John and I discussed ways for him to learn how to control his frustration better when his peers tried to make him angry.

While I was working and following up weekly on stage one of the action plan that had been discussed in the session, to see if the physical bullying had stopped, the second part of the action plan was still to be implemented: speaking to the school.

During a session, we discussed the action plan for the school meeting, including how follow-up would be done. I discussed that his mother and I would meet with the principal to discuss the program that John was in and the serious concerns about John wanting help from the adults and their responses to him. John felt good about the questions his mother and I would ask. He also indicated that he felt his voice was already heard by the adults and would rather have his mother and I talk to the principal without him. (Note: Some children will be in the room when parents are meeting with the principal, but others would not do well in a school meeting. We'll talk through how to know whether to include your child in a school meeting, such as this, a bit later.)

I made sure John was clear on the action plan and agenda going into the school meeting. I explained that his mother and I would advocate for him, requesting that the adults respond better and help John if the physical bullying continued. I assured John I would let it be known that John's voice was important to be heard.

The day of the school meeting arrived. John's mother and I reviewed the agenda for the meeting right before we went in to see the principal. The principal and vice principal both came to the meeting. John's mother spoke first about why she'd called another meeting and her concern for the continued bullying, which was becoming physical at times. The school let us know they'd thought all the bullying had stopped. John's mother explained that the bullying was continuing daily.

I then validated John's mother's concerns and went on to discuss different strategies and plans we had worked on with John to help him deal with his peers. John was doing his best to learn and take in the skills. However, the one area in which he did not feel supported was by the adults at school.

The rest of the meeting was spent coming up with an action plan that would involve following up every few days with John at school and making sure his coach or teachers and the vice principal were checking to see how the situation was going.

We also agreed that John's mother would be in touch with the principal within a few days to see how the other adults were now responding to supporting John. I suggested the mother contact the vice principal once per week to make sure the reports John was telling her were consistent with what he was telling the vice principal. There would also be a weekly discussion to address any needed changes to the plan of action (of John choosing to ignore his peers and not respond to the bullying). The vice principal agreed to weekly phone calls with John's mother and a monthly in-person meeting with John's mother and the principal.

The vice principal would be on the lookout, along with the aides and teachers, to make sure there was no bullying occurring, that they could see.

We all agreed to a progress meeting one month later, to see if the physical bullying had decreased.

For the next four weeks, John's mother and the vice principal talked weekly and reviewed the bullying from the previous week. She talked to John and the other teachers. John's mother also checked back in with John after the meeting to let him know that the adults would be working on better ways to communicate, and that they supported John and would help him out and intervene if necessary.

At the next meeting, John reported that the bullying had gone down and that he was feeling now that the adults would intervene and advocate for him.

We decided to de-escalate the engagement. The vice principal would call John's mother once every two weeks, and would schedule a third in-person meeting with John's mother and the principal one month later. We continued the check in, but the frequency decreased as John's bullying was lessening.

At the third meeting, John reported that the bullying had all but stopped. John stated that once in a while, the kids would try something, but he now felt more confident in what he was doing to stop the bullying and if this did not work, he felt the adults around him communicated that they truly supported him.

In the example above, there were two plans of action. There was one relating to how John chose to respond on his own with his peers. The second plan involved John appealing to the adults and compelling them to respond in a positive manner to him.

The consistent follow through with John and the vice principal seemed to make a huge difference in the plan working. The specific engagement in this example was daily check-ins by John's mother asking how things were going. At least weekly, John and his mother would speak to the vice principal. There were monthly meetings with the school principal until the bullying stopped. The specific plan of action was the follow through, that the adults would better communicate ways to help John when he came to them. They would make sure John saw in their actions a change in their responsiveness to his being bullied. Engagement requires consistent follow through. That means daily or every few days at home with parents, depending on the severity of the bullying, and weekly with the school.

In the example above, if John's mother had decided to follow up with John only once in a while, or if the school had stated they were too busy to be bothered with weekly check-ins or monthly school meetings, and said they would meet only when necessary, this would not be positive engagement for John, who was being bullied daily. The school and the parents needed to be working together consistently in both environments to see a change in John's physical bullying.

Effective engagement follows up

Engagement is following through with your child's plan to cope with the bullying and consistently checking in with your child, the school, and any other people involved assist in executing that plan.

Parents often confuse engagement with saying that they talked once or twice to their child and then felt the conversation was over. Parents get busy in their own lives and often have more than one child to take care of. It is not easy for parents to check in with their kids daily. They will do the best they can, given their own busy lives.

This sort of "extreme" engagement, daily check-in with your child, weekly check-ins with the school, and monthly meetings, may be a challenge, but know that it is short lived. This kind of check in will not be forever and may make a huge difference in stopping the bullying. And it will certainly make your child feel more supported.

I know that you have your own busy life, but I also know the serious concern that I have, given how your child is feeling because of the bullying. Do your best and think through some samples of time frames and amount of follow through that you can commit to. Maybe you feel like you can check in with your child on Mondays, Wednesdays, and Fridays. That's okay, but do commit to talking with your child on those days. Maybe you can't have a school meeting every month, but you can have a meeting three times during the semester. That's okay, too, but put those meetings on the calendar as soon as possible.

Engagement is the most important part of the Three Es, because this is the step that will ensure the bullying has stopped. It is vital to have both empathy and empowerment with your child, but the follow through and engagement will make the difference for whether the bullying will stop.

The accountability surrounding children being bullied is huge. Adults, like those in the example above with John, need to be responsible to children who are feeling unsafe. In John's case, everyone worked together like a community, to each take a part to help John with the bullying. If adults are not accountable, then the children will not feel safe.

Engaging the right people who can support your child is very important when you follow-up on a plan. In the example above, it was important to not only bring in the vice principal, but the principal as well. It was important to have the vice principal understand, with the support of the principal and John's mother, why his approach and that of the other adults had not been working. John's mother felt she was not successful previously in communicating her concerns to the vice principal, and that some form of miscommunication had happened (as was felt by John).

Empathy and empowerment are the necessary foundation to engagement.

Begin at the beginning. Have a discussion with your child, once you have learned about the bullying. It is important to use the empathy strategy to gain a closer connection and understanding with your child. Also, open-ended questions are important to make this connection successful.

The next step, once your child's feelings have been validated, is to discuss a plan of action. Once you and your child have agreed on a bullying action plan, then you can begin to engage.

The first step to engagement: establish a regular check-in with your child

The idea of consistency means different things to different people. Some people will be able to do daily check-ins, while for others it may not be possible. But the idea is that some regular plan of follow-up is important to make sure things are getting better. It may be easier for kids to tell their parents they are fine and let the conversations stop. But, it is still important for you to sit down and really explore your child's thoughts, whether she is better or whether she needs more assistance. It is your job to model what follow through will look like in your household, and you must hold your child to this. Give her the schedule of what time and how often this will be. If you plan to check in with her every day at 4:15pm, tell her that. If you plan to check in with her Monday, Wednesday, and Friday at 8:15pm, let her know. Set it up as a planned meeting, just like any other meeting, and hold that space for your child.

Consistency with follow through around bullying can look different for different families. It can be very close and regular, as with John and his mother, or it may be more spaced out, depending upon the time that is realistic for parents to spend really talking to their child on a regular basis. In the example with John, his mother felt comfortable with daily check-ins with him, and this seemed to be a level of comfort for John as well. But not all children are as close or connected to their parents. It depends on the connection with your child, but regular follow through is still important and can bring you closer to your child.

If you see your child start to act less depressed, seem more happily engaged in activities with others, and seem as though her self-esteem has increased, this may mean your child is feeling better about herself. Regular follow through will still be necessary to make sure that the bullying is really gone. It is all about the honest connection you have with your child, to allow her to disclose her thoughts. Still, having conversations from time-to-time by asking open-ended questions such as, "I am wondering, are you still feeling better? If there is anything you may want to share with me, I am here for you."

I will use the example of John and his mother with a sample dialogue of engagement:

> *Mother: Hi, John! How did it go today at school? Did the other kids try to push you or get a rise out of you?*

John: Yeah, they still tried but I ignored them.

Mother: That sounds great. How did you feel ignoring them when they were trying to make you mad?

John: It was fine. I did not care that much.

Mother: John, can we discuss other scenarios for you to use if things get worse, and your options of what you can do?

John: Sure.

The next day while John is on the computer:

Mother: Hey John, how was your day? How did things go at recess today? Did anything upset you?

John: A few kids just made some stupid comments, but whatever.

Mother: Well, let's just review things you can do in case things get worse, for a few minutes after you get off the computer.

This would continue regularly, though perhaps not as formally, and may be at the dinner table or before sitting down to a family activity. It can be done as a check-in and can be casual. It does not always need to be a formal time to check-in, but should still be consistent to make sure things are truly better.

We never know how long bullying will last. It is hard to put a time frame on bullying. It can go on from year-to-year and day-to-day and may never stop. That is why the engagement phase is so important. If you and your child have a plan of action and follow-up regularly for a period of time, chances are better that the bullying will decrease and there will be more open support for your child. Even after you've helped your child cope with bullying, you'll want to continue to engage your child at key milestones, such as:

- Before a new school year
- When starting a new sports team
- Before school trips or retreats
- Before drop-off for social events that might not have school or parent supervision

There is never clear reassurance that bullying will stop for sure. But having the relationship with your child that shows support and guidance will lead your child to want to confide in you. The connection that can be made through the framework of the Three Es (empathy, empowerment, and engagement) will help build a strong connection to your child, maybe even a closeness you haven't experienced before in your relationship.

The second step to engagement: set up a school meeting and agenda.

There are two parts to the Three Es framework. The first is using all three parts together to have meaningful conversations with your child. The second part is bringing the Three Es to the school. How do parents and their child handle the school being involved if the bullies attend the same school? How much should the parent intervene with the school to help support the child? There is no right or wrong answer to these questions. You may or may not have an understanding of your child's school climate or environment. How has the school previously handled issues and how supportive have they been in hearing and addressing concerns? These are the first questions parents should ask themselves and their children about the school. In asking these questions, I do not want to deter you from approaching the school officials. Rather, I would encourage you to learn how to have a good strategy going into the conversation.

I spoke to a parent the other day who had gone to the vice principal of the school and felt that she and her daughter were not receiving the support they needed from the school. Then, when they went to the principal, they started to feel heard. This gives them good information about who should be part of a school meeting.

My suggestion is that you approach the school from the top down. This means it is important to have the principal or vice principal in the meeting in their school building, and, if you need someone even higher up, to ask the superintendent to join the meeting at the school. It is also important to include a teacher who really knows your child and seems very supportive of him. A teacher or other member of school faculty will be the cheerleader of the group and a positive role model on a daily basis for your child.

I would also ask to see a copy of the school's policy on bullying. If there is no school policy on bullying, I would ask to see the policy on harassment. This will also give you a better idea of the school's procedures for teachers to handle these issues.

Before suggesting a school meeting, both you and your child should agree that another plan needs to be put in place with the school. You want your child to buy into the idea that talking to the school will be helpful for her. Once you get your child on board, it is important to talk to your child about a plan for the meeting.

The agenda of the meeting should include who will be present, what will be discussed, interventions for change, and follow-up, with another date to meet again. I recommend meeting monthly. Once the agenda is discussed, you should call the school to set-up the meeting and request at least the vice principal and the principal to be there, along with other relevant people, such as teachers or coaches.

Then, it is important to discuss your child's thoughts on the plan of action. I would start by asking your child for her suggestions and then possibly role play how this plan will play out in the school office. An example would be:

Parent: *"What are some important things that you want mentioned in the school meeting? What would you feel comfortable saying?"*

Once the meeting has concluded, it is important to review the discussion with your child and the specifics of the follow through plan. Also, check in to see how she is feeling. As discussed in the case with John, follow through is daily or every few days with your child. Follow through should be direct weekly with the school, until things are getting better.

Here is a template you can use when planning the school meeting agenda:

1. Two weeks before the meeting, request to see the school's policy on bullying so you can review before the meeting.
2. One week before the meeting, make sure all necessary teachers, and vice principals are present that can support you in the meeting.
3. Just before entering the meeting, make sure you as the parent are calm. Take deep breaths if needed.

4. Once you begin the meeting, thank everyone for being there and let them know you as the parent really want to work with the school.
5. Review the school's bullying policy, as a group.
6. Explain ways you are addressing the issue with your child at home.
7. Ask for suggestions with how they can support you further at school with the bullying.
8. Come up with a clear plan in writing.
9. Identify at least two to three interventions. (i.e. The vice principal will speak to the parent weekly. The teachers will intervene when they see the bullying take place. The teacher's aides will support your child in asking for help.)
10. Ask that an e-mail is sent after the meeting either by school or the parent with the agreement of the plan discussed
11. The school will respond and agree to interventions by stating they received the e-mail.
12. Schedule another meeting within the next month to see if everyone identified for an intervention has followed the plan, as detailed in the email.
13. Thank everyone in the meeting again to make sure the feel of the meeting remains collaborative.

The third step to engagement: follow up with the school personnel, concerning the discussed interventions.

You will have to be the one who sends emails to the school and makes sure the personnel respond that they've received the email. You will have to be the one who calls the vice principal weekly. You will have to be the one who sets upcoming meetings to discuss your child's bullying situation. The sad truth is that if you, or your family therapist, does not engage with the school personnel, your child's bullying situation will not remain a priority for them. And, through it all, I still recommend that you attempt to be as collaborative as possible with everyone.

Being collaborative with the school

I had a parent call me up not too long ago and ask if I would go into the school where her child was being relationally bullied and speak to the administration. The mother had already gone to the school and attempted to be collaborative, but she did not feel that it was working. She asked me how I would make a stronger approach to the school. I told the mother that it is never a good idea to approach a school with any focus that does not start out as collaborative. If I did not attempt to gain the trust of the school and the officials there, I could not help her make headway. Although she had tried several times herself and felt she was not getting anywhere, the key was that I, as an outsider, could go in as a neutral person. I could attempt to suggest a collaborative relationship that would hopefully allow the school to hear the concerns and feedback better than from the parent.

The mother understood my stance on a collaborative relationship, at least for the beginning of how to address them. She understood that if I went in extremely headstrong or with threats, this would not help her or her daughter, as schools tend to be wary of the presence of a therapist, especially one that comes in part way through the discussions.

When I accompany parents to school, I make sure that I show in my manner, tone, and actions that I am there to really work collaboratively. I ask open-ended questions, just as I would with a child. I ask the principal, "What would you recommend to stop the bullying and keep this child safe?" And I continue the dialogue until we have a concrete, detailed plan of action that we all feel good about. I do not want the school to see me as an enemy. I want to gain the trust and understanding of the school personnel over time. My intention with schools is to have a collaborative relationship where we work together to support a common goal.

I make sure that the school knows that weekly follow-ups will be crucial, as well as monthly meetings, to really stop the bullying from happening. The commitment for follow through with both the parents and the school (daily and weekly), make all the difference in giving a child real hope that change can happen.

I was in a meeting a few weeks ago at a school whose officials I hadn't met before. I went in with a friendly demeanor, knowing that a friend of mine, who has a great organization to help kids with bullying, had spoken at their school. I let the school know that this person was a friend of mine and how wonderful it was that he'd come. When the school heard this, it was the first step to engage them positively with me as a therapist, and with the process. I also gave them praise for their support in a situation with my client. I think my openness and willingness to work with them made the school officials relax and launch into on finding ways to help my client with bullying.

School follow-up can vary from place-to-place. Some schools have more resources and are able to invest more in helping kids address bullying. Every school has a different culture.

I had a school meeting a few weeks ago with two teachers for a client named Samantha. I introduced myself with the mother present. The teachers were witty, smart, and very attentive to my client. As they spoke about Samantha, I understood immediately how much they liked her. I could sense by their tone and body language that they were invested in Samantha. The teachers were easy to work with and asked to hear about my strategies for addressing bullying in my program. The teachers even asked for specifically worded phrases I use and skills that they may be able to incorporate at school. They are always kind when we meet, and they make enough time to really address the bullying. I walk away from each school meeting smiling about the positivity and follow through that these two teachers show.

Whether it is with the parents, therapists, teachers or school personnel, we all need to work together and help children heal from bullying. I really feel it does take a village and without the school's support, this would be a much harder task.

Should your child attend the school meeting?

Once the date of the meeting is set, it is important to see if your child *wants* to attend the meeting. As the parent, you can strongly encourage your child's involvement in the school meeting. You can empower him that his words in the meeting matter.

But if your child is strongly against being in the meeting, we do not want to re-traumatize him. If he does not feel comfortable going to the actual school meeting, empower him to tell you what he would like to be said, on his behalf. Make sure he still provides you with what happened to him and what he wants the school to know. Also, make sure if he has any suggestions for solving the bullying that these thoughts are also brought to the meeting.

The way your child is still being empowered is by making sure his voice is heard. Whether this is in-person or through the parent. Empowerment is still taking place as long as your child's thoughts, ideas and words are being voiced in the actual meeting.

Children may not feel comfortable being a part of the meeting, but it is important that he knows his voice needs to be heard and that the adults will make sure of this in the meeting.

Parents bring their own painful memories onto the campus

You may feel it's best for your child to be absent from the meeting, but I'm afraid you'll have to be there, and you may find the meeting more emotionally difficult than you might first expect. If you feel angry with a school and hurt by your child being bullied, I think this reaction is very understandable. You try to help your children as much as you can, using you own coping skills, but if you were bullied as a child and can identify with your child, you may have very strong memories that have started to resurface. Those memories may intensify as you walk down a school hallway, with lockers and classrooms on either side of you. Know that it's okay to feel whatever you feel in that moment, but remember that it's in your child's best interest to collaborate with the school.

One parent, whose child was in my program, had previously experienced bullying herself. I attempted to use her own experiences of bullying to get her to validate her daughter's feelings in a more empathic manner. I tried to use her own feelings to elicit empathy and understanding for her own daughter.

You may find that you are able to go back to these painful places in your own life and talk about your own experiences of bullying. You may find yourself pushing those memories under the rug, so to speak, and trying to forget your own pain. I do not want you to feel any shame, but I also want you to see your part in how you can make situations with your child better.

You may be able to help your child with his pain by understanding your own painful memories. Being open and vulnerable with your own childhood stories can make the empathy, empowerment, and engagement approach with your child work much better today.

A special note on engaging cyberbullying

Adults often cannot catch cyberbullying. All you can do is change how your own child reacts and responds and teach your child how to take a screen shot of the person making the threats.

The only way to engage a school in cyberbullying is if the IP address of the student shows that he or she attends the actual school. Then, you could show the principal a screen shot as proof. Most schools, depending upon the state laws, would then be liable to intervene, even if the actual bullying occurred on a social media site and not on school grounds.

Please make sure to get a copy of the actual policy on bullying to see how it may apply to your child's cyberbullying.

I'd like to share a story from a child, who was enduring fierce cyberbullying. When I first met Joseph, I could see on his face a great deal of stress. Joseph's father, Rick, had called me regarding his son being cyberbullied.

When I met with Joseph and Rick to address the cyberbullying, I introduced myself to Joseph. He told me he had recently come out as gay and was still having a hard time with this. He also told me he was getting threats on his Social media account and was starting to get worried about attending school.

Here is how I used empathy, empowerment, and engagement to address showing Rick how to use these skills to help his son with cyberbullying:

> *Rick: I'm glad you told me about the cyber bullying. I am wondering if it was hard to be here today to talk to me and the therapist together. I know I mentioned that you are being pretty severely cyberbullied by other kids, to the point of being scared. I have such empathy for you. I am wondering if you are feeling very hopeless right now given how hard it was to come out alone and now getting increased threats. You know as your father I support you and accept you.*

> *Joseph: Yeah, it is hard. I am trying to accept my sexual orientation and then with others not embracing me it is hard.*

> *Therapist: I know I cannot take your pain away, but I think your dad and myself can work on better ways to help you cope and not react to their threats that will not give them any unnecessary attention.*

> *Joseph: I guess. I really do not say much to them.*

> *Rick: Can we talk about a plan to handle future threats being made to you? What are some thoughts of a plan you might want to use?*

Joseph: I am not sure at this point.

Therapist: How are you responding or engaging with others on your social media sites?

Joseph: I am just putting pictures up of me and my boyfriend having fun and commenting on other pictures.

Therapist: Ok do you happen to know if the kids sending you mean comments attend your school or you can identify who they are?

Joseph: Yeah some of them I recognize.

Therapist: How would you feel about taking a screen shot of their comments?

Joseph: I guess, but I do not want more problems.

Therapist: I understand that we do not want to make the situation worse or escalated. But if they are threatening to harm you, we need to know this.

Joseph: Well, then what do I do?

Therapist: What would you like to do and what would feel comfortable for you?

Joseph: Nothing.

Therapist: Are you feeling that if you ignore them they will no longer do this? We cannot change others but we can work on a plan of how to help you better handle yourself with social media and not responding to their comments and if it gets more serious take screen shots of their comments and go to the school with this information?

What about a plan of action to role-play ways to better engage on social media by not responding to them or possibly blocking them from your pages? We can also role-play situations of how to better handle yourself when your peers are trying to cyberbully you. What would this be like as a plan to start?

Joseph: I guess but I am not really responding now.

Therapist: That is great and we will work on better ways to help you handle any further threats that come up. This may include talking to the principal of the school.

Joseph: Ok.

Therapist: The final part of this will be the follow through of the plan with your dad and myself. I will be seeing you weekly and your father will check in nightly to make sure that we can tweak any changes that are needed.

Engagement with cyberbullying relies on your child buying into the plan and seeing that there's no benefit to doing nothing; the bullying can only change if your child agrees to let you know when it's happening and takes screen shots of the social media posts, texts, and emails.

A special note on engaging relational bullying

Relational bullying is tough because, again, adults typically do not see it and it is hard to stop. The best way to support your child is to help her adjust to the situation and provide empathy of feelings, empowerment of how they would like to meet new friends in a plan of action, and engagement to follow-up and show caring and support that they do try other things and ways to meet more people who will treat them better. You may ask a teacher to help you keep tabs on your child's relationships with her peers, but you may need to continue following up with sample dialogue above for as long as you still see your child as depressed.

I would actually caution you against engaging the school unless it becomes necessary and the relational bullying is so extreme that your child is experiencing a deteriorated school performance, fear of attending school, or throwing up because of anxiety. It is important that you speak to your child first about calling the school and letting her come up with what she feels comfortable having you disclose. Many kids can face the risk of retaliation from the bully or bullies if adults get involved. If there are ways that as a parent using your own empathy for your child coming up with a plan of action such as above and follow through of the engagement that would be the best thing to do. If you feel alone, please seek the help of a family therapist.

I will never forget the day I first met Victoria. I had received a call from Victoria's mother, Marion, regarding relational bullying that she was experiencing at school. Victoria, who is in the 9th grade, has a physical disability with a limp. Marion, has worried for years about Victoria's physical disability causing problems for her daughter with her peers. In the past, Victoria has had a hard time making friends, but in the last year has met two girls who have befriended Victoria. Victoria usually has the friends over to her home. Every week the girls are usually going to each other's homes to hang out.

Recently, Marion noticed Victoria was no longer having her two friends over and overheard Victoria talking to a peer about not being invited to her friends' houses for a party recently. Victoria was in tears on the phone as she relayed the story to her friend.

Marion started to hear Victoria cry much more at home, usually secretly in her room. A pattern developed of Victoria seeming to be left out of activities by the two friends that she had always hung around with.

Marion had access to Victoria's social media account and found that there were other events Victoria was being left out of and suddenly both of her friends no longer wanted to hang out with her.

I received the phone call from Marion to help her deal with the relational bullying her daughter was experiencing. Her daughter was all alone and isolating from others quite a bit, and seemed to now have no friends anymore. Victoria was not wanting to go to school and was throwing up every morning when she knew she had to attend school.

I talked through a sample dialogue of how to use empathy, empowerment, and engagement with Victoria and her mother:

> *Marion: Victoria I am wondering if you feel hurt by the two friends that no longer talk to you? I am wondering if you feel very alone right now?*

Victoria: I guess so. I thought these two girls were my friends. I have always had a hard time making friends because of my stupid limp. People have always called me names.

Marion: I am so sorry this has happened to you. Kids can be cruel when they do not understand something that may be different about someone else.

I am worried about you and how depressed you have become since the girls started leaving you out and stating they no longer want to hang around with you and chose to be with other girls who made fun of you in the past. How would you like to address the relational bullying that you have experienced?

Do you have any specific ways that would help make you feel better? I would like us to come up with a plan. Your father and I would like to see you feeling happy again.

Victoria: I'm not sure how to change the situation. They are not calling me back, leaving me out of activities and pretty much ignoring me at school. They will not even respond to my text messages.

Marion: Are there other kids you may want to talk to? Is there a way you can do other activities and meet other kids to help with finding new friends? Is part of the plan looking to see through activities or your classes other kids you may want to hang out with? I cannot imagine all kids at your school would not want to hang around with you?

Maybe other clubs you can join where people may have similar interests. What about making a plan to try and find one activity this week that you may want to try and meet new people. I can role-play some dialogue if that would help?

What if as part of the plan we make a list of the qualities you would like to find in friends and we work on helping you through practice and role-play to meet new people?
I know this does not make you feel better about the two people you thought were your friends. How are you handling when you see them with other kids? Can we role-play ways to help you feel you have more control in these situations if you start to feel sad such as walking away, writing in a journal, ignoring them with others.

Victoria: I am not sure what activities but I will try.

Marion: That is great. Your father and I will follow-up with you on how making new friends and your sadness about missing your friends is going. I will find a time nightly just to do a check in and see how the day was for you. It is important that we hear your voice, because what you say is important and has value. Your dad and I will keep reminding you about this every week and help you to make sure you start to feel better and know there are other friends out there for you.

Victoria: Okay, sure. Thanks, Mom.

Even if you are the only one following up with your relationally bullied child, know that your empathy, empowerment, and engagement can help you to be a true champion for your child

The power of engagement

As the summer of my fourth-grade year came to an end, I started getting really scared. I knew that the day was coming soon when I would go to school and look on the board out front to see who my teacher was going to be that year. Would I be able to make some new friends, or would people remember bullying me from last year?

The first day of school arrived. I was nervous and scared, my hands sweaty. I wanted to cry but was being as brave as possible. My mother walked supportively by my side. Before I could reach the board where I was to find out who my teacher was, a little girl with short, curly hair came up to me and said hello in the friendliest voice. Her name was Lisa. She was not a friend who had been in previous classes with me, but I knew who she was. Her friendly voice made me relax instantly. She asked me who my teacher was and stayed close by my side, along with my mother. I introduced her to my mother, and they exchanged hellos.

I then went to the board to see who my teacher was. Lisa's kindness made me feel that maybe things were changing. I was hopeful that a new year and friends were coming. I hoped that Lisa's positive engagement would only be the beginning of making new friends.

Lisa's kindness and excitement put my mind at ease. I felt that I had a new friend who did not care about the previous bullying I had experienced.

The idea of engagement with people is a powerful thing. I wondered if this was for real or a dream.

Chapter 5:
Putting the Three Es Together

———◆◆◆———

In the past three chapters, we have learned about the Three Es: empathy, empowerment, and engagement. In each chapter, we took each concept apart, and learned about examples and sample dialogue demonstrating how, as a parent, you can use each concept with your child.

Each concept is important in learning how to talk to your child about bullying. These chapters serve as the beginning to understanding the Three Es. But I believe *this* is the most important chapter, since I will now illustrate how all three ideas of empathy, empowerment, and engagement work together to make a successful dialogue with your child happen.

Empathy, empowerment, and engagement all work together like a well-oiled machine. The first step is to approach your child with an issue using open-ended questions and reflective statements such as, "I am wondering if you are feeling angry about the comments made about you on your Instagram account?" Remember that you need to be in an appropriate emotional state, free from distractions and stress. Your tone of voice and body language are as important as what you say.

Once you go to your child in an empathic manner and are able to understand how he feels, you and your child can discuss an action plan to handle the bullying. Discuss and empower your child to come up with a plan of action using guidance and suggestions from you. A statement that empowers your child may be, "I want your voice heard by the school, so let's share some thoughts you might like to say to the principal? I know we discussed that you will be staying off your Social media account for a while and will not be responding to any peers making mean comments. Is this something you would like to share with the school? I want to make sure your voice is heard."

Empower your child to come up with plans of action and help him come up with initial ideas, if he is depressed or beaten down by the bullying. It is important to be emotionally present with your child when you approach him with empathy, and it is important for you to bring positive energy to empower him through an action plan.

The final step discussed in the last chapter was the follow through or engagement of the plan. It is important to have weekly follow-up when the bullying is actively happening. Weekly follow through with your child will be important, as is having a time to check-in. An example of dialogue for engagement and following up on the plan would be, "I am going to put a time on my calendar to check in next week with you to see how the physical bullying is going, plus I have a phone call scheduled with your vice principal next week to follow-up on any further concerns as well."

All three of these concepts work independently, but together they synthesize into something truly powerful. Here is a quick re-cap of the steps for all Three Es:

Empathy

The first step to empathy: listen your child's feelings without judgment.

The second step to empathy: mirror your child's feelings.

Empowerment

The first step to empowerment: ask your child about a plan to handle future bullying and create a bullying action plan together.

The second step to empower your child: role play the bullying action plan.

The third step to empowering your child: check in with how your child is feeling about the bullying action plan.

Engagement

The first step to engagement: establish a regular check-in with your child.

The second step to engagement: set up a school meeting and agenda.

The third step to engagement: follow up with the school personnel, concerning the discussed interventions.

I developed the framework of the Three Es after significant research and training about what works most successfully with children. If bullies and the victim are brought to the office together, and the bully is penalized, most likely the victim will be re-victimized. Alternatively, positively encouraging the victims to come up with solutions to bullying can change the entire relationship. Empowering children to be positive is what seems to be the most successful method in handling the bullies and making sure the victims stay safe.

Each component of the Three Es approach requires you to talk with your child about bullying. Each part is important, but together, they address the issue of bullying comprehensively.

Let's walk through an example of the way the Three Es of empathy, empowerment, and engagement can be used together.

I had a client that came to my office named Maggie. Maggie was a 12-year-old, shy girl who was suffering from intense verbal and relational bullying at her school. The girls at her school would pretend to be her friends and invite her over to their homes. Then, at the last minute, they would cancel with her and make sure she would hear from those same girls that they actually did get together without her. They would laugh about it in front of Maggie. Recently, Maggie's supposed "best friend" started engaging in the relational bullying and would ignore Maggie and exclude her from plans. In short, the 'best friend' stopped having anything to do with Maggie.

Maggie's mother Shannon sensed that the relational bullying was intensifying and getting worse because she would hear Maggie crying in her room. Shannon also had parental controls on her social media account and could see on the account e-mails that Maggie desperately wrote to these girls she thought were her friends. Maggie's mother brought Maggie in to meet with me after seeing an increase in depression, social isolation, and excuses that she did not want to go to school. Maggie's appetite was also decreasing; she refused to eat most dinners.

Maggie would spend a lot of time in her room, sleeping. Shannon and Maggie's father felt helpless and very worried about their daughter's increased depression and isolation.

Maggie was open to coming to individual sessions with me. In the first few sessions, I built up my rapport with Maggie, finding out who she was, and what motivated her and made Maggie actually feel good. Did Maggie feel she had hope for the future? We worked on her self-esteem and strategies to help Maggie come up with a more positive sense of self-worth. Maggie and I practiced role plays to help work on better responses to address the relational bullying.

Our fifth session came, and I wanted to help Maggie's parents to start talking to her about the bullying, using the Three Es. In the session, I practiced with the family how to use empathy, empowerment, and engagement together. There were also follow-up activities that they would be working on together. Here is how the conversation went at home to address the relational bullying.

Shannon: Hi Maggie. I wanted to check on how you are feeling right now working on the bullying. I am wondering if this is bringing up more sadness for you? Are you feeling it is helpful? Where are you with everything? It is important to me to hear how you are truly feeling. Your thoughts matter to both me and your dad.

Maggie: It's going fine. I am learning different strategies.

Shannon: So, am I hearing that you feel this program is helpful? I would really like to hear a bit more on your thoughts if you are comfortable sharing this.

Maggie: Yeah, I like it.

Shannon: I am glad to hear this. One of the things we discussed is coming up with a plan to handle the relational bullying when it happens at school. What are you currently doing to handle the problem?

Maggie: I'm just ignoring them.

Shannon: Are you still responding to their text messages or answering questions that they ask you on social media?

Maggie: I guess so.

Shannon: I am wondering if we can sit down for a few minutes to discuss a different plan to help you better handle the girls at school when they try to say mean things to you. It sounds like we may need to add more to what you are already doing. But I want you to be part of this plan and feel good about what we decide to do.

Maggie: Okay, I guess.

Shannon: I'm wondering what it might feel like to not only ignore them, but not let them know through your responses that they're getting to you? Possibly, we can role play different responses you could give to them to show they are not bothering you?

Maggie: I guess they usually just laugh in front of me.

Shannon: How about we try a few role plays right now to show different responses? Also, how do you want to handle social media? Are you thinking that not responding may be more helpful? Let's come up with a plan on what you would feel comfortable doing in this situation.

Maggie : Okay, but really mom, I can do this myself.

Shannon: I know you can handle things yourself, but I want to help you feel less depressed and sad by the current responses you are giving to them. I want to see less sadness from you. I want to support you, and not tell you what to do. I want to support you in just fine-tuning some of your responses online and at school. Does this make sense?

Maggie: Yeah, I guess.

The plan was decided and Shannon practiced role plays over the next few days on how to better handle the interactions with the girls at school. Shannon is doing her follow-up plan in this discussion.

Shannon: Hey, Maggie. How about after dinner tonight we spend some time talking about how our plan is working with your responses to the girls at school.

Maggie: Okay. I am busy now, but I guess a few minutes after dinner is fine.

Shannon came back into Maggie's bedroom for the next few weeks every other night, checking in with Maggie and doing some fine-tuning of the responses she gave to the girls at school.

Maggie checked her social media account and talked to her daughter, and found that she was getting closer to her daughter by consistently finding time to talk with her, usually at night after dinner. It started to become a ritual for them. Maggie's dad also started being part of these discussions, which had never happened before. Slowly, Shannon saw less isolation from her and that Maggie was making better choices with how she was responding to the other girls. Slowly, Maggie found other friends at school and was not giving any power to the girls who were bullying her.

Shannon would continue to follow-up with Maggie regularly, since the bullying did not die out completely and would still happen occasionally.

As the therapist, it was great to hear that things were getting better for Maggie. Even at the school meetings, there were less reports of Maggie isolating from others. They said that Maggie seemed to be engaging with a new group of girls. It seemed Maggie was doing better, and yet all agreed that watchful eyes needed to stay on Maggie, since the bullying had not stopped completely.

The parents found the Three Es to be helpful, a new road map in which to feel powerful with their child instead of feeling powerless. It gave Maggie's parents a way to really address the bullying, depression, and social isolation. Maggie's parents did feel they needed to use their own words and dialogue that would work for them, but found the road map given was a helpful, new approach to looking at bullying.

It is important that you, too, buy into using empathy, empowerment, and engagement consistently, with your child and with the school. If you truly give the Three Es a chance to work, they will. If you have one foot in and one foot out, there will be less success. If you make the commitment that change is needed and that you will give full attention to the plan, you can see remarkable changes in your child.

As we saw with Maggie, her parents watched her slowly decline into a depressive state, but they knew they could make a change. Maggie's parents were willing to invest the time and effort to really help their daughter feel better. They no longer wanted to feel powerless.

If you use and follow through with all components of the Three Es, you will hopefully see a decrease in the bullying. The bullying may not go away completely, but it will decrease. This can also give you and your child a chance to have better communication with each other. The concept of the Three Es provide better, honest, and direct communication with your child. You'll gain a better understanding as to what is going on with your child, and not leave you feeling left out of their lives.

With time, the Three Es will help your child learn how to communicate better with you and others. It will allow him to feel empowered, that his voice does matter, and that there is support and guidance from you as the parent to help him address the bullying. If nothing else, it leaves your child feeling less lonely and less isolated. It allows your child to have a voice again, both with you and his peers. It shows that your child does not need to be alone with his sadness, that your child has people around him who care and really want to know the truth of what is happening. It allows your child to see that he is not burdening you or worrying you. He sees that you will not be angry with him. It gives a new outlet for change to occur and a sense of hopefulness to shine.

The hope is that with better and clearer candid conversation, your child will not feel she needs to be alone with bullying. She'll feel she can have the support around her to be empowered and that her voice does matter to others around her. It will hopefully show her that silence and isolation is not the way to feel better; pretending the bullying isn't happening will not make it go away. It takes courage for your child to ask for help and to acknowledge that she cannot do things by herself.

The consequences of unhealed bullying

As a speaker, I go to many different places to give presentations on bullying. One of the issues that consistently arises is how being bullied as a child will affect you as an adult. I will usually ask for a show of hands for how many people in the room still get triggered by bullying as an adult. Usually most, if not all, hands go up.

Occasionally, I will have a person from the audience approach me after the presentation to discuss the pain and anguish that continues into adulthood. One man I will always remember, recently came up to me and stated that he still gets triggered daily by the intense verbal and physical bullying he experienced as a child. He feels small and powerless, even as an adult now. It has affected his interpersonal relationships and abilities to advance at his job. He finds himself getting very sad and lonely all the time. He feels stuck as the adolescent boy who was horribly bullied. He does not feel he can get away from the deep and intense feelings of not being good enough.

As I heard his story, I felt sad. It reminded me again why I do the work that I do: so that we can use strategies, self-esteem skills, and coping skills to help children heal from bullying, with the hope that as adults they do not feel continued pain.

There are many adults I see in my practice who are still emotionally paralyzed by the bullying they experienced as children. They have a hard time letting go of the pain and are very afraid to feel it now as adults. They hope by not revisiting this painful place, that all the anguish they feel inside will go away, but this never happens. Childhood bullying will manifest itself when you're an adult if it is not addressed. We still carry the negative childhood beliefs into adulthood. The pain is as fresh as the day it happened. If you are a person who is still feeling tortured by the bullying you felt as a child, it is important to get help. Seeing a therapist or psychologist can be very beneficial. By going back to the childhood memories, you can heal previous pain and help increase your self-esteem. It can also be helpful, as parents, to heal your own childhood bully wounds so you are able to take your knowledge and empathy to your children and understand their experiences of being bullied.

As someone who as a child experienced bullying for years, I know the feeling that you are not good enough. I know that constantly comparing yourself to others can be devastating. It can be a continuous angst that does not go away. As an adult now, I still get triggered by situations and feel less than others and not good enough. Although I got help, my self-esteem always feels sensitive. That painful feeling never goes away completely. That is why I feel hopeful with the framework of the Three Es.

Then I go back to my fifth-grade year. I start to remember the pain. The first day of fifth grade happened. I was slow to warm up to my new classmates for fear of how they would treat me. I found out that the ring leader who bullied me had left the school. It was amazing how overnight, with that one powerful bully gone, my entire environment had changed. It changed how others viewed me.

I remember having a fifth-grade teacher who believed in me. He believed in my voice, and that what I said mattered, and told me that I was pretty smart. I remember a project that I did that year. My teacher was big on group activities and children working together to learn. I got paired up with this other girl in the class who sat close by me.

At first, it felt uncomfortable to work with another female peer my age. I was worried about what would happen. Did she remember how I was bullied from the year before? We started going over to each other's houses to work on the project and we slowly became real friends. She embraced me as her friend and took me into her home and family. Up until then, home to me meant watching TV or playing with dolls while a babysitter looked after me, since my parents worked long hours. I finally had a place to truly be myself.

Our project did very well, but more importantly, I gained my first real friend after the fourth-grade bullying. I slowly felt the anxiety and fear slip away. I felt like I could relax and start to be myself. I wonder, if I had had the Three Es as a child to help me, would I have been better prepared for a new positive friendship? At the time, I wondered if this was only a momentary chance of friendship and if I would continue to be bullied...

Chapter 6:
Healing Tools: Self-Regulation and Self-Care

———————— ➤ ◄ ————————

Remember when Lauren and her parents had come for their final session together? We had worked for 10 weeks with Lauren and her parents, and all of them had made tremendous progress in helping Lauren to deal with her bullying situation. Lauren was happier, smiling more, and said she was optimistic about being able to cope with the bullies. Our conversation was supposed to focus on the progress we'd made in the program, as well as support and encouragement for Lauren's growth, but her parents' emotions were running high and running the show.

As the session started, I discussed some ways that Lauren had addressed the bullies at her school during the week before. I remember immediately the energy in the room changed from one of excitement and happiness to one of silence and sadness. It only took a few minutes and a few words spoken to change the entire mood from one of happiness to frustration and complete disappointment.

But Lauren's parents were having a very hard time regulating their own emotions, thoughts, and tone of voice toward their daughter. Lauren had hidden from her mother the fact that the bullying was still going on. Lauren's mother's face had fallen and then tightened up in anger. Lauren's father looked stunned, seeming to shrink in his seat with his eyes looking off in the distance. I could see Lauren closely watching them and knew that she didn't see their feelings, didn't understand them. She saw only disappointment and anger with her. I watched Lauren helplessly fall victim to her parents' frustration and anger about the continued bullying. I had compassion for the parents and their feelings. I could see they were upset that the bullying was continuing, fearing for their child, and hurt that Lauren hadn't disclosed this information to them. They felt that the bullying might never stop. I could also see the tears that were slowly welling in my client's eyes.

I watched the parents struggle with emotional regulation and the ability to hold their fear and frustration at bay, to try and understand why their daughter did not disclose this information to either parent. I watched the struggle in the parents' tone, their body language, and their attempts to convey their hurt and fear that the bullying continued, as well as the inability for their daughter to feel safe in coming to both of them.

I watched first-hand the results of the parents' inability to regulate their own emotions around bullying and how this affected my client dramatically. I am not faulting the parents or their attempts to be compassionate, but because of their emotional responses, the outcome left nobody feeling better.

The excess of uncontrolled emotion by all in the session left an unhappier family, who did not feel as connected after the session or in the mood to celebrate this important moment.

Not only does this kind of excess of unregulated emotion leave the family feeling unhappy, it also unintentionally victimizes the child. Even if the parents' words show support, if their tone and body language felt angry, their child will feel pained all over again, as much pain as she does when she's bullied by other kids.

It is important for you to be aware of your own approach when you talk with your child about bullying. We want to make sure we are not adding more fuel to the already existing fire.

What I have seen over 20 years as a professional in the field, is that when parents are calmer and more present with their children when they approach difficult topics such as bullying, it will lead to a better, more loving outcome and connection.

Check your body language, tone, and timing

When having a conversation with your child, remember that he is paying very close attention to your non-verbal cues. In fact, 90% of human communication is non-verbal, which means that your body language, tone, and even timing will absolutely determine whether your conversation with your child is successful or not.

Bad body language might include being hunched over, not making eye contact, frequently looking away, holding your body very stiffly, or sitting rigidly upright. Instead, stand tall, ready to make positive eye contact, and hold your shoulders back in a secure manner.

Also consider your tone of voice. If the words you are saying are supportive but the tone is very angry and frustrated, your message will not be received. If you *feel* angry, you probably sound angry, too. A good tone will come through if you are feeling calm. Your voice should sound light, with no intense feeling. You need not only to be calm, but to also show this with your voice.

As for timing, it is important to read the room when you walk in to talk with your child. You need to sense whether the mood of your child (and yourself) is in a non-distracted and calm state. If your child is distracted, frustrated, or angry, it may be a bad time to approach her.

Remember, when you enter your child's room to read the social cues: Are your child's shoulders relaxed? Does he seem tense or frustrated? If so, you many need to try engaging your child in a fun activity that brings down his defenses.

If you are not sure how you will come across, try role playing with a friend or another parent to practice how you might want to say things to your child.

When emotions run high

Usually when parents first hear about bullying, they are worried and angry. Parents want to defend their children and do not want to allow others to hurt them.

You will need to strengthen your own abilities to self-regulate your emotions and feelings—which is not always easy. You will need to refrain from sharing too much of your own thoughts and feelings with your child, in order *to show your presence* to your child. Be there for your child and show her you are ready to listen to her. This does not mean being unauthentic about how your child's bullying situation is affecting you, but it does mean remembering your child will already be concerned about not wanting to burden you or worry you.

You will need to find a way to regulate any anger or frustration you have in order to not be overly emotional. It's fine to admit that you are upset, but you must keep the anger to yourself and deal with it separately, when you are not with your child.

When you first find out that your child has been bullied (whether it is from your child, one of his friends, or a third party), I suggest the following steps to taking care of your own emotional regulation.

Step one to self-regulate: feel your own feelings.

Be angry, cry, shout, call a friend, or speak to your spouse about the issue. Please, have your feelings. It is very important as the parent that you allow yourself to honestly feel that what has happened to your child is very upsetting at the least. If you do not allow yourself to have your feelings, then you may get so flooded with your own emotions at another time, that you may not be as helpful to your child. It is important to allow yourself the time to grieve over what has happened, and to feel all of your own emotions. Please do not skip this step.

Step two to self-regulate: take some deep breaths.

Think about how you might want to approach your child with the information that you know she's being bullied. You may want to speak to your spouse, the other parent, a friend or a therapist to address how to effectively approach your child about the bullying. That is a very important question you want to ask yourself. How can you effectively talk to your child and feel that you are not showing your own level of frustration too deeply? How can you make sure that your child will not worry that you will be mad or that she is causing you pain?

Once you have calmed down and asked yourself how to approach your child with the information about her bullying, then it is important to speak with your child directly. Before you speak to your child, you may want to role play with your spouse, another friend, or therapist about how to say things and how to get your child's feedback. Find someone who is not highly reactive or who will trigger your response to be more upset. Speak to someone who is even-tempered and not emotionally invested in your child's situation.

Even though the bullying should be addressed as soon as possible, it may be even more important to wait a day or two (or more) until you feel more able to have a thoughtful way to have a conversation with your child.

Step three to self-regulate: engage in self-talk.

Lauren's mother was caught off guard by the realization that the bullying had continued, but I think if Lauren's mother had been able to use more self-regulation, she may have been able to engage in what therapists call "self-talk."

Self-talk is just what it sounds like: talking to yourself to prepare you for what lies ahead. An example of self-talk might be, "I know I am really upset and frustrated right now that this bullying is continuing, but I am going to keep my voice calm when I ask Lauren questions, and I am going to be careful that my tone and body language is not accusatory. I will speak very even-keeled and keep the emotion out of my voice."

There will be times when you have no idea and are blind-sided by the bullying. There may be times you will be caught off guard. I think it is important that even at those times you do some self-talk, saying, "I know I am upset right now, but I will take a few deep breaths and try to hear my child without judgement. I will further address this topic when I feel truly ready to be present with her."

It is not always easy to do this kind of self-talk in the moment, but I encourage trying to do this, if you feel your own emotions could get in the way of an important conversation with your child. You need to learn to listen to your inner voice and the importance of repeating, over and over again, that you and your child will be fine.

Self-talk is really just to help you remember to self-regulate your emotions, and it is good practice because sometimes you may not have the luxury of having time to prepare your responses when you learn about bullying. It will take practicing self-control and self-talk, along with deep breaths, to truly manage the appropriate tone of voice and body language.

Self-talk is an important tool for parents to use. It is important that as adults we begin to have an internal dialogue with ourselves that shows we can decrease our anxiety. Using self-talk to regulate your emotions with positive self statements can help. This would look like: "I know I will be okay. I can do this even if I am feeling angry and frustrated." Using self-talk while taking deep breaths or taking a walk will help with better self-regulation of emotion.

In the example above, Lauren's mother was not new to her daughter being bullied. If she had been able to do more self-regulation in the moment and quietly own her frustration, would this have led to more opening up of dialogue between her daughter and herself? The bigger picture always needs to be in your mind as the parent. What will my frustration and anger do? Will this lead to a better conversation with my child that will help him or her feel supported, and able to come to me with her sadness around being bullied?

These thoughts are important. Having a big picture perspective on the issue and the outcome that you desire will be very important. Your child needs to see in your body language, tone and voice, as well as manner, that you CAN handle his emotions. *What he feels is not too much for you.* He needs to see that what he feels is important, despite all your responsibilities and needs as a parent, and that you are completely present with him in the moment you choose to talk with him.

It's okay to be human

There is no perfection required to use the Three Es or to always being emotionally present.

Bullying is an emotionally charged topic that can bring up many triggers. It's a hard topic to discuss. The idea of another person causing such deep and intense pain is hard for others to hear.

When you hear that your child has been hurt, all you want to do is protect her any way that you can. Your own anger can get in the way and not allow you to see clearly the bigger picture of how to help your own child. Your own emotions and feelings, rightfully so, will get triggered, but you need to discover the self-awareness to identify when you're triggered and how to bring your emotions back in check.

Self-awareness is not always an easy skill to gain. This means we take time to really look inward at yourself, your thoughts, and your feelings. Take stock of your own reactions to situations. This is not easy and takes time, but the importance of self-awareness means you have power to change your own behavior and are not powerless. The awareness will give you the guidance needed to be more aware of your actions.

Parents make mistakes, as we all do. If in the moment, like Lauren's mother, you are not able to hold together your own feelings of frustration and anger, that is okay. It is most important that you go back to your child later, to own your mistake in how you engaged in the discussion. Then, you can let your child know you now are ready to hear her. Remember, children do not care if parents make mistakes—it is the correction of the mistake that children will remember.

As you learn to better regulate your emotions, you'll get better at taking care of yourself—and vice versa. To give you a good idea of what self-care is, let me give you an example of how things can go wrong when it's missing.

I counseled a man, Steven, who was in his 50s and came in quite depressed and beaten down. He smiled when he met me but I could tell even a small hello was a lot for him. Steven had been diagnosed a few years prior with an autoimmune disease. He had two children and had to move home with his adult parents. Steven could not work due to his symptoms and was having a very hard time raising two children while living under his parents' roof. The client explained that daily living with his family was like a slow death to him. His parents treated him like he was a child again, and always had negative comments to make about him and his children.

Steven had full custody of his children and struggled to make ends meet. He truly felt trapped by both his disease and the negativity in his parents' home. He did not know how to manage himself or his two children. His oldest child had issues related to the home situation, and moved out on her own, while his teenage son was still living at home and was being physically bullied by other kids at school.

He came to therapy, which had been recommended by his doctor, to help address his son being bullied and to address the various stressors that he was facing.

When I sat down for my first session with Steven, I could feel his sadness and hopelessness filling the room. After we explored his story and situation, I asked him, "How do you take care of yourself? Do you have self-care practices?" Steven gave me this look of confusion, "What are you talking about? What is self-care?" I replied that self-care is how one takes care of and prioritizes their own needs. This may be getting a massage, attending therapy sessions, going for a run, taking ten minutes nightly to meditate or read a book before sleep. Self-care should usually be repetitive rituals of an action done to help you relax and center yourself. He then told me how he did not have time for this between going to doctor's appointments, talking to the school about bullying with his son, and trying to mend his relationship with his daughter.

I could see at that moment that this client truly had no idea how important self-care was, or how to implement it in his life.

Steven had no idea how to do anything special for himself that would make him feel good. He explained that his existence became about daily survival and getting things done. I believe many parents share Steven's feelings that life is already too busy and constrained to try to "fit in" anything like self-care. But stay with me for a moment, and I may help you see self-care in a new light.

> *Self-care makes empathy, empowerment, and engagement possible*

If you're not practicing self-care, you won't be fully present to support your child through this difficult time of a bullying situation. First, let's talk about what self-care looks like, then why it's so important for the empathy, empowerment, and engagement that we've talked about in this book, so far.

There are different aspects to self-care: the first is knowing that you *have* needs, the second is being able to identify those needs, and the third is being able to *ask* for what you need in order to truly take care of yourself.

I have a friend who regularly walks in the evenings when she's stressed out and gets massages every two weeks. She explains that with her high-powered job, she needs to walk to clear her head, and she needs the massages to make sure she is loosening up her muscles that get tense from the stress. This is an example of someone who is aware of the need for self-care and can identify productive ways to take care of herself.

An example of this would be a mother I know who makes time every week to have a date night with her husband. Each week this parent gets a babysitter on Saturday night so she and her husband can go out and enjoy themselves. Whether this is dinner, a movie, massages, or exercise classes, it is about three hours of relaxation, allowing them to come back feeling refueled. When she is confronted by an emotional situation with her children, she has the emotional calm to be open, and to listen with empathy.

Weekly self-care may be hard, but finding something you can do consistently will help you feel better about yourself and, in turn, allow you to be more present with your child.

To Steven, who has a serious illness, lives with his parents, and has two children with issues including one who is being physically bullied, the idea of self-care is a foreign one at best. This is not a parent who has been able to understand the need for this, in order to continue to endure his many stressful situations.

Steven exhibited no awareness of the need to take care of himself. All he could think about was survival. He did not believe he was any danger to himself or his children by sacrificing his own needs for the sake of his children and his illness. He was coming into therapy only to consult with me about his son who was being bullied. He did not for one second think about coming to therapy to talk about his own issues and struggles.

I think the idea of simple survival is a common one among parents. They feel a need to just get through the day and that may be a success to them.

But is this truly *living?*

Self-care allows you to be more present for yourself and your children. If you do not take care of yourself, then the ability to be present and available to your child, particularly with one who is being bullied, will be much more difficult. When you have a child who is being bullied, it is very triggering, physically and emotionally. It is important to be helpful to your children, to be able to show through your actions how you take care of yourself. Modelling self-care is important to your child because he needs you as a guide; he needs to see how to care for himself as he maneuvers through the landmines of bullying.

Children will learn from you that self-care is important. As a parent, it's not always easy to be a perfect model, and I hear a lot from parents who say that taking care of themselves is not always possible. However, if children see that you can take care of yourself, and regulate your own situations, your child will see that as a sense of strength, showing that you can handle your grief and hurt. When you take care of yourself, your children will be better able to self-regulate their emotions, too.

Self-care is self-compassion

I see many parents who are much better at being compassionless than compassionate to themselves. I find parents are very hard on themselves and sometimes their own worst critic. But you should not only take care of yourself, but also be kind to yourself. The self-critique can easily eat away at you if you are not careful. It is much easier for you to judge yourself harshly rather than give yourself a compliment.

In the example above, Steven was easily able to talk about all the negative things going on in his life, which were valid. Yet, he also was very critical of the job he was doing as a single parent. It was hard for him to find anything positive that he could say or even do for himself. I had such compassion for the difficult life circumstances that my client had been dealt and how hard he was trying to make things right with his children. I felt sad that my client had no idea how to have compassion for himself, or ways he could acknowledge what he was doing well.

Self-compassion means understanding that you have a hard situation and finding ways to say kind words to yourself without being overly hard or self-critical. It is being able to find ways to look at the positives of what you provide to yourself and your children. It is truly giving yourself a break: letting go of some of the baggage.

What would being self-compassionate look like? It would be Steven understanding that he has a hard and stressful life, but still acknowledging he is doing the best he can to survive daily. He can congratulate himself that he's there to help his children, and can let go of the actual mistakes that he may have made. He can let go of his inner-critic and instead be forward thinking and positive, understanding that life happens and can be very messy.

If you as the parent cannot let go of your own self-critic telling you that you're not good enough, how will your child feel? Children learn so much from observing how their parents live.

If you cannot let go of your own negative inner voice, then how can you model a positive self-image for your child? You want your child to have good ego strength. You want your child to feel good about who he is, and while bullies already try to push victims' self-esteem down, you want to do the opposite. You want to model that we all need to give ourselves a break and cannot be the perfect person every moment.

Children need to see you take care of your body, mind, and feelings. If your child does not see you as a strong person, with positive self-esteem, she may feel a lack of safety to come and share her thoughts and feelings. Your child may fear burdening you or making you further worry about her.

It is very normal to experience extreme feelings of anger and frustration if your child has experienced bullying, for years or even recently. You may say the wrong thing to your child, or you may make a mistake. As the parent, you may say something in frustration to your child about how to handle a bully, but that's okay.

It's okay to make mistakes

I tell parents all the time that I encourage them to make many mistakes. I actually encourage parents not to feel they need to be perfect, because children do not care about the number of mistakes you make; they care about the correction of the experience. Children remember how their mom, dad, or guardian fixed the mistake and went back to process the situation. Children remember the outcome of how the situation was addressed. They want to know that parents have imperfections and, even with these imperfections, can acknowledge this in their manner, tone, and body language, and can own what happened and how they may want to do things differently.

Parents, when they make mistakes, usually get angry either at themselves or their children. They may yell at their child or overreact to a situation and then ground them harshly.

If this kind of situation happens, it would be important to go back to your child and say something such as, "I am really sorry that I grounded you for the entire week, and once I learned that you did not say those things to your sister, I should have come back and apologized sooner. I made a mistake and I hope you can forgive me." This is an example of taking responsibility, owning that you are not perfect as the parent, and telling your child you are sorry. This is giving your child a corrective experience.

Is your child going to screw up a lot? Of course. Show your child that it's okay to make a mistake and that mistakes can be corrected. What a wonderful learning opportunity, for both you and your child!

Finding the support you need

We all need support and love. We cannot do things ourselves and be successful without support of some kind. In the example above, I was surprised by how much and for how long this father had done so much himself and I could see in his eyes, his body language, and manner that he was struggling and needed some support.

Find support in friends, family, other parents, support groups, or even a therapist to talk to. It is important that you have one person in the world who listens and provides love and nurturing to you. The father above felt so alone in his pain, both physically and emotionally, that he had no true connections of support and nurturing.

You cannot do things alone. You cannot be a parent and worker, all in one. You need to have help, and that is okay. The form of support can look different for people. Not everyone needs the same thing, but the key word is to "need" support. It is important for you as parents to reach out to other people who love and respect you for support.

I feel the most strength is found in people who can ask for help, in people who are not afraid to be vulnerable and know that they need other people to survive the uncertain world that we live in.

I think about my own support system and how important each friend is to me. I know that the world is a better place for me because of my friends. I can be myself, and I know even with my many flaws they will still be there for me when I fall. As friends, we can be there for each other and that is part of the deal. If one of us has a bad day or needs support and we comfort each other, we say thank you for being able to provide the support we need.

People, like Steven, who do not have support will drown emotionally. If he had waited any longer to come in for support, I wonder if something worse could have happened to him. He was so beyond emotionally and physically burned out that he had no sense of anything. He felt so hopeless and helpless, believing that life would never get better.

Depression can lead us to scary places and thoughts of suicide. It is important to create a support network that works for you, or you may find yourself sinking into a deep abyss of depression.

You are alone in the world, with all the messiness and wonder that comes from being a parent. You need to feel that you have others on your side to help you stand strong when you cannot do this alone.

When you take good care of yourself and gather the support you need around you, you show your child how important it is to find good friends.

I think back to the end of my fifth-grade year. I had begun to make friends who were there for me. I knew they truly had my back. This was the first time I understood what true friendship looked like. I had friends who would stand up for me if someone else was teasing me. I also started having better self-care. I participated in activities that made me happy and enjoyed my time with friends. It was so nice to finally meet some friends who were protective of me and our friendship. Having someone else who cared about me and appreciated the qualities I brought to the friendship made me smile inside. The sadness that I had from the summer before was slowly moving to pure bliss and excitement, for what was to come after the summer and when I started sixth grade.

For the first time in a long time, I was excited about summer and felt like a new person inside. I was grateful for the friends who now stood up for me when I was bullied.

Chapter 7:
The Three Es in Context

———➤◄———

When I first bring in a family and begin working with them on empathy, empowerment, and engagement, I sometimes hear some pushback, especially from the parents. They say, "Our family is different. We don't talk to each other that way," or, "People in my life won't understand dealing with bullying this way." So, I want to take a moment to address some of the concerns and doubts that may be riding in the back of your head.

It's true that not every family, every school, and every community will use empathy, empowerment, and engagement in quite the same way, but you and your child can show up to the conversation in your own way.

When you or your child isn't a "talker"

It is important to start where your child is. If you do not usually talk about feelings with your child, then you need to think about some ways you would feel comfortable talking to your child. You could practice the idea of empathy by asking a simple, initial question, "I am wondering how you might be feeling?" You can use those exact words to attempt to get him to really start talking to you. It may feel foreign to you but could be helpful. I would suggest trying out a question that starts with, "I wonder if…." and then add a feeling you think your child may be feeling.

For instance, "I wonder if you are feeling upset right now because of something that happened to you today?" This is a good place to begin the conversation. You aren't so much trying to talk about your own feelings as you are opening space to listen to your child.

Some children, especially teenagers, appear too busy or preoccupied to sit down for a conversation. Maybe your son plays video games or skateboards. Maybe your daughter likes to spend her time at a friend's house. I would suggest you engage in one of these activities with your child or at least drive your child to and from activities with minimal distractions. The best way to really talk to children is to meet them where they are at, so maybe join in the activity. Then, while you are doing the activity, it may feel less threatening to check in and ask an open-ended question such as "I wanted to check in and see how you are doing. How are you feeling?"

When parents aren't on the same page

It's very common that one parent is more concerned about bullying than another parent, and the differences may partly be due to experience. Maybe Mom remembers being treated meanly by a group of girls and being traumatized by it. Maybe Dad remembers being teased, and he says he just "ignored them." Maybe one parent has never experienced any bullying. Likely, each parent will have a different approach to their child's bullying situation and will not be on the same page.

I would suggest that both of you have a real heart-to-heart conversation about the importance of helping your child always share his voice. It's okay for one parent to take the lead in having regular conversations and follow-ups with your child, but if the other parent is constantly undermining the seriousness of the bullying, it will be difficult for your child to feel safe and heard. You may consider bringing in a therapist to help make sure everyone's opinion is shared.

All parents' situations are different. Parents do not all intervene or think about things in the same manner. There will be differences in home situations, such as divorced parents, single family homes, or parents who are together, as well as situations where parents living together may be on separate pages. All of these are viable situations and can make the follow through different, but the roadmap and guidance of concepts will remain the same. All three Es need to be used consistently and with follow through, even if the dialogue and manner in which this happens looks different.

When extended families have different opinions

It's common for grandparents and people from older generations to have a gruff response to bullying. They may suggest just letting the kids "handle it" themselves, insinuating a physical confrontation, and such comments may make it difficult for you to stay on the path you've set with your child.

You may need to have a serious conversation with extended family to explain that your child is hurting and that you are thinking of the best ways to deal with the root of the bullying. Don't be afraid to ask others to be respectful of the way you are raising your children, and don't be afraid to have a heart-to-heart with them and to share how painful the process has been for you.

When life is busy

Making time for conversations with your child, your partner, other family members, the school, teachers, and your child's peers can start to feel like a part-time job. Maybe you work late nights or two jobs. Even so, with technology today, you could have a FaceTime chat, or perhaps a conference call.

Certainly, a conference call can be scheduled with the school, if you cannot go to the school to actually speak to them during work hours. You can put something in the calendar to remind you of the upcoming conference meeting. It is important to show your commitment to collaborating with the school, even if this needs to happen by phone.

When you're the only one who wants to try the Three Es

Since you're the one reading this book, you may feel like no one else in your family is ready for this change, but you are. Let me reassure you that you can bring on the support you need.

I'd like to share a story to address this issue. I had a client, Jane, who was 12 years old. Jane was very close to both of her parents and felt safe coming to them about any issues that she may have had. Jane's mother, Elaine, had come to me to address physical and verbal bullying at school. Elaine was a very attentive parent, kind and extremely loving with her daughter. She was caring and protective and did not want her daughter to be in pain anymore due to all the bullying she was experiencing at school. In the first session, I went through with Elaine the expectations of the program. I defined each person's role and expectation for her and her husband to come in for three sessions to work on empathy, empowerment, and engagement.

As I was explaining this to Elaine, she briefly interrupted me to say I could not expect any participation from her husband. They were very happy together, but her husband would not participate in any of the program, and did not believe in therapy or a program to help kids with bullying. Elaine was clear that she and her husband had an agreement, and that he would handle certain responsibilities with Jane and her brother, and Elaine managed other things.

Elaine turned to me in the first session very directly and wanted to know that I clearly understood this. Inside, I was crushed. I really want both parents to attend the sessions and participate with children who are being bullied. I feel that the parents do a disservice to themselves and their children when they actively choose not to participate in a program that may be beneficial to their children, as well as to themselves as parents.

Elaine explained that in her culture, she did not question her husband, who believed that bullying should be handled by Jane and that she should defend herself, including using physical aggression, if needed.

I listened to her words carefully. I replied that I understood the situation and asked open-ended questions such as, "How do you feel handling the entire program yourself?" She explained that she had been the one parent handling Jane's education and therapy for years, and that her husband and she were fine with this understanding. I asked her what happened if Jane went to her father regarding issues surrounding bullying.

Elaine explained that her daughter had a clear understanding of who she could go to for certain issues, and this system had always worked in their family. I listened to the family dynamic and agreed that I would do my best to work within their limits to try and help Jane heal from bullying.

In time, Elaine, Jane, and I found a nice balance working together. Elaine was very attentive and would actively participate in any activities or assignments, in order to help her daughter.

I had to use the Three Es effectively in the above example. I had to be reflective immediately and empathic to the situation at hand. I needed to come up with another plan of action that would work, knowing the father would not participate in the program. I then had to create situations where we could still empower Jane with the support of Elaine, as we followed through on the action plan.

I learned a valuable lesson in this process. I had this belief that if there were two parents in the same home that they needed to work together in order for there to be any success for their child. I learned through Elaine's strength and tenacity that we were still able to help Jane heal from bullying, and that Elaine's role still made a huge difference in the success of her daughter.

Couples may not always agree on how to handle situations, but as the therapist, I try to hear how each person feels and work within the framework I am given. In this case, allowing myself to come out of my comfort zone and hear the needs of this family was not only therapeutic for them, but myself as well.

If you're ready for a change, you'll make it work

While all of these concerns (and any others you may be thinking about your own situation) are entirely valid, the truth is that if you feel your child and your family are desperate for a change, you will find a way to make it work. You'll find the time to have the conversations, you'll put yourself in the uncomfortable position of starting a conversation with your teenager, you'll breathe deeply, and keep trying.

The approach and presentation of the Three Es will look different, but the ideas of empathy, empowerment, and engagement all happen within communities. It may look different depending upon the way in which each community engages with its members and with each other, but I do believe in the end, all families, schools, and communities have issues around bullying. Indeed, bullying is a behavior that crosses race, religion, and socio-economic status. It does not discriminate; all kinds of kids are bullied, though it is true that some kids are bullied because of their race, religion, or privilege.

Before you know it, you'll be encouraging empathy, empowerment, and engagement in all of your relationships, and that sounds like a beautiful consequence.

Chapter 8:
Positive Peers

Empathy, empowerment, and engagement do not just have to come from a supervising adult. Peers have tremendous effects on each other, as well. Your child's peers can show in their actions, tone, and body language that they are sincere and want to help your child get through a hard time. In fact, if peers empower other peers to support them while the bullying is going on, it can have a huge impact on an adolescent.

I had a 15-year-old female client, Gloria, come into my office. Gloria came in to talk through some issues she was having at school. She seemed surprisingly confident and well-spoken. As she shared her story with me and her feelings about her situation, her maturity, and passion, blew me away. She was an artistic person who was quite involved in her art program at school. Gloria told me that she had recently experienced a series of situations where a good friend of hers was being bullied. The friend was very special and dear to Gloria. While initially, it had seemed that Gloria and her friend were very different, over time she came to understand and appreciate the differences they had. Gloria knew her friend reacted to some situations in ways perceived as strange to others and although others may not understand her, Gloria had found common ground with her friend.

Gloria told me that there were several instances when she would be around this friend and other peers (since they all had classes in common) where her friend was being teased. A pattern was forming in which this was happening every day during a math class. Sometimes the teasing was subtle, and other times it was very direct and clear. Gloria would hear the other kids whispering about her friend, making mean comments about her, or ignoring her. Every time this would happen and Gloria was asked to join in (They might say, "C'mon, Gloria, you know it's true!"), but she would decline. Gloria would turn to any set of the peers and tell them they were being mean, even though they were her friends, too. Over the years, as this behavior had been ongoing for a long time, Gloria would call these peers out and stand up for her friend even when her friend had no idea the joke was on her.

I was struck by how strongly, with conviction, Gloria consistently took into account her friend's feelings and not for one second ever let her friend get mistreated in front of her. Gloria looked to me to help her understand why this mean behavior would ever be tolerated by anyone, because she did not understand this.

Positive, neutral, and negative bystander

Bystanders are people who are in the area when a bullying situation is taking place. Bystanders will either negatively or positively affect the bullying situation, in particular, how the bully will behave. The bystander will either join with the bully or set themselves apart and can change the dynamic instantly.

A **positive bystander** is someone like Gloria, who can positively change a bullying situation. Positive bystanders can stop the behavior of the bully by not going along with their negative behavior, and can actually make the behavior positive and turn it away from the victim.

Sometimes, there are more quiet bystanders who may not be outspoken in their defense of the victim, but may still silently oppose the bully. They may not necessarily stand up for the victim vocally, but they do not engage in the negative behavior of being mean. This is considered a **neutral bystander**. They are not actively being negative or going along with the mean behavior, but are not proactively standing up for the victim, either.

A **negative bystander** is a person who can negatively impact a bullying situation. The negative bystander will vocally go along with the bully and encourage mean behavior, standing with the bully to hurt the victim. Negative bystanders are so mesmerized by the bully and so fearful of being bullied themselves, that they will not be able to act any other way. If Gloria had gone along with the mean comments and harsh behavior towards my client's friend, then she would be a negative bystander.

And that's exactly why the bystander is truly the most important, powerful person within a bullying situation. The bystander has the power to change the situation into either a more negative one or a positive one. The dynamic between the bystanders, whether it be just one other person or more, can change how much power and attention the bully gets. This person can change how the victim is viewed.

A positive bystander can change the situation into a positive one. Gloria was regularly goaded to join her peers in being mean to her friend, both behind her back and in front of her, but who chose not to engage. Instead, she actually turned the situation around to the point of criticizing her peers for having the audacity to say such cruel things. Her strong and secure confidence led her to change the situation by standing up, and supporting her friend consistently when others would put her down.

By taking a stand and letting the bully know that their behavior is unacceptable, the positive bystander changes the entire situation. A bully will no longer have the power, given by their peers, to be mean. The dynamic changes, the bully loses their power, and usually the bullying will then stop.

Being a positive bystander needs to be something that a person innately feels is the right thing to do. Children learn how to be a positive bystander through modeling in the home by their parents, as well as their own morals, ethics, and self-confidence. Gloria felt that there should never be acceptance of mean behavior. She truly did not understand the reason for the mean behavior, and she would not allow it to continue to happen in front of her.

On the surface, the benefit of being a positive bystander is simply to stop children from being mean. It makes a statement, both verbal and nonverbal, to all nearby, that it is possible to have the strength and courage to be kind to others. Seeing positive bystanders empowers children to be good people who have compassion and love for those in their community. The more positive bystanders we can encourage, the kinder and more accepting we will become as a society.

The Three Es, empathy, empowering others, and engagement, connect quite well to being a positive bystander. The power in the positive bystander is to have the courage to be empathic and to understand that your friend's feelings are being hurt, to empower your friend through your own conviction of truth, and to follow through with, and holding to, the refusal to allow others to be harsh and cruel to your friends. All three parts of the Three Es can be found in a positive bystander.

I have watched over the years, situations in which the bystander changes the dynamic with a bully and victim. I have seen children as bystanders hurt each other and contribute to more of the victim's pain. I have also seen children who are willing, like Gloria, to be courageous and have the strength to not go along with the crowd. Some bystanders remain connected to their own beliefs about right and wrong, and do not sway the other way.

Helping your child to become a positive bystander

As a parent, it is important in learning the Three Es that you also empathize, encourage, and follow through in supporting your children to be positive bystanders. You can strongly instill an understanding of what is right and wrong in a situation.

Because you know the difference between what is acceptable behavior and what is just being mean, you can show your child that empathy and understanding another's pain is a valuable life skill. You can teach your child that it isn't normal for teenagers to regularly put down or tease others.

You empower your child through your parenting to be good people. What a "good person" is may mean different things to different people, but the essential component is to be a kind and loving person who does not hurt others. If this behavior is modeled well in your home, then your child will understand the importance of what being nice looks like. You instill the values of being a kind person, and you can encourage your child to always stick up for others who cannot defend themselves.

Have an honest dialogue with your child about how important the role of the bystander truly is. Most parents talk specifically about being a bully or a victim but do not regularly discuss the bystander role. Empowering your own child to do the right thing means leading your child to come to their own understanding of what he feels is right and wrong. It is important that you hear your child's thoughts first before intervening or trying to change his mind. Even though being a positive bystander is powerful and noble, it's important to realize that if you teach your child to stand up and not go along with the bully, your child runs the risk of being shunned by their peer group or bullied himself.

This means you'll need to be there to support positive behavior. You can role play situations to help encourage positive behavior when others are being mean. However, the truth is that we can encourage children, but they will ultimately make their own decisions.

It can be hard to be a positive bystander. Peer acceptance is the most important thing for children, and peer pressure is strong among children. Everyone wants to feel they belong and if a person stands up against the group, there is always the fear of being ostracized. Many kids will tell me that it is easier to go along with the bully than to stand up for the victim. The children become worried that their own reputation and friends will be put at risk. It takes a great deal of courage and ego strength to stand up to one or more peers who are being the bullies.

Bystanders can stop the bullying if they are clear in their actions and statements, that they do not care if they lose their friends, that they would rather not have bullies for friends, and that it is more important to them that they are not involved in mean behavior. In fact, many children default to neutral bystander because they feel so scared and worried about their own reputation and friendships, that even if they do not agree with the mean behavior, they will go along with it silently in order to stay in good standing with the bully.

There have been experiments done where some parents think their kids will stand up for a child who is being bullied, but when the re-enactment or video is played back to them, they are surprised to see their child go along with the bully. The power of peer influence is huge and can scare many children away from doing the right thing. Ultimately, a positive bystander has to have a strong conviction and be fearless of peer pressure, or the outcome of any victimization he or she may experience in order to stand up and stop the bullying behavior.

Stand for the Silent

My friend Kirk Smalley, who provided the foreword for this book, founded an organization called Stand for the Silent. The Smalley family's story is powerful. Nine-year-old Ty Smalley was bullied for two years, until he finally retaliated and was suspended from school. Despite his mother working at the school, despite both of his parents loving their son, at eleven years old, Ty took his own life.

Kirk has taken his son's bullying story to the masses, in order to raise awareness that bullying is an epidemic in our schools and has extreme consequences, even for the kids we try to convince ourselves "will be okay." Kirk does the most powerful presentation for children on how to stand up for the defenseless kids. He empowers children with his wisdom, strength, and conviction, inspiring children to take a positive stance. I have watched a room of 500 children listen to Kirk and then completely own their strength and power in standing up to bullies. The champions against bullying like my friend Kirk Smalley make the difference for kids to be a positive bystander. His ability to speak to a large audience and have a powerful impact on them is pure genius.

In supporting the Three Es, parents must work on their empathy for understanding the challenges your child may face with peer pressure, and the fear of being socially outcast in his attempts to be a positive bystander. Next, it will be important to empower your child to learn and model ways to stand up for others who are being victimized. Then, help him to create a plan of action for being a positive bystander and engage him in the plan.

Discussing the following questions with your child can help with a follow-up plan:

- How will you stand up as a positive bystander?
- How will you get out of your comfort zone to support the victim?
- What will this look like?
- Will you consistently stand up for the victim?

You can support your child in doing the right thing, and the best you can do is attempt to utilize the Three Es as a roadmap of guidance for how to encourage your child to become a positive bystander.

I remember vividly how good (and scary) it felt to be a positive bystander as a child. It was the first week of my sixth-grade year. I was actually excited to go back to school. I had a group of friends I was starting to feel safe with, and I was hoping we would all be in the same class, but it turned out that was not to be. Would not being in the same class pull us apart? Without my good friends in my class, how I would get along with my other classmates? Fortunately, I made new friends in my class and learned to adapt to my environment.

One day, a student in the class was giving a presentation. He was a bit uncomfortable in front of the larger group, but he was doing his best to speak with confidence and conviction. Part way through his presentation, some kids who sat behind me started making fun of him. At first my heart skipped a beat because I feared they would do the same thing to me when it was my turn to give a presentation. I asked myself whether I should turn around and give them a clear dirty look to stop, or should I wait for the teacher to say something.

I could see the peer giving the presentation was starting to feel more uncomfortable and I could see his face begin to turn red. Slowly, without any further thought, I turned around and gave these two kids the nastiest look. And that was all it took. Suddenly the kids behind me stopped making their mean comments.

I saw myself go from being a victim of bullying to a positive bystander. In that one moment, I was able to stand up for this kid in my class. Why? Because of the friends I had met, who had the strength to see me differently than the bullies did. I wanted to now pay it forward to other victims of bullying.

Chapter 9:
The Empowerment Space Program

———————▶◀———————

Thirteen years ago, I was on my honeymoon in Hawaii. I was with my husband, sitting outside on a June day, eating breakfast and reading quietly in the beautiful sunshine and calm of Hawaii. In the magazine I was reading, I came across an article about bullying, and was instantly interested. I turned to my husband to share the contents of the article, and he said, in a very loving and supportive manner, that I should use my skills to support victims of bullying.

It was not until ten years later that I was able to make my passion a reality. I will never forget his words that day near the beach, in the most calming place in the world. They helped me begin this healing journey that I hope you too have been able to join. Allow me to tell you the story behind this book.

I was working at an insurance company doing inpatient authorizations for hospitals. I would get calls from facilities requesting that the insurance company, based on clinical information, give the patient time in a behavioral unit in the hospital. I started getting many calls for adolescents who were trying to kill themselves. When I would regularly ask about the triggers, for the need to authorize an inpatient stay, the facility would explain that this was due to a child being bullied. Sometimes, the kids only made threats to hurt themselves, but there were also times that children would actually try hurting themselves, trying to die.

Over the six years I worked there, I started to see a clear connection between children hurting themselves and bullying as the cause. I would ask facilities I worked with across the country what kinds of programs they had to counteract the increase in reports of bullying and inpatient stays in hospitals. Many of the facilities I worked with had varying forms of school programs. Not one had a community-based clinic that worked with children at the crisis point, *before* needing hospitalization.

I began doing more of my own research and learning about what programs were out there for children being bullied within the community. I did some work with a few non-profits and learned more about the world of bullying.

However, I did not feel this was enough. Three years ago, I commissioned an independent consulting company to do a needs assessment within my local community in California. They researched what resources were out there for children who were quite depressed but not to the point that they required hospitalization. The needs assessment took three months to complete. Within the time of the needs assessment, educators, parents, therapists, children, community leaders and other experts in the area of bullying answered questionnaires and interviews.

At the end of the three months, I was presented with a written report on the findings. I was told there were no community-based clinics that specifically addressed bullying at the crisis point. There were prevention programs in the schools, and therapists who would address the issue of bullying with their clients, but there were no specialized treatments specific to addressing bullying as it was happening.

Based on my vision and the under-served needs I confirmed through this assessment, I was told that I would need to create my own program and do a pilot study. And based on the results, I would then look for funding to build a community-based center.

I spent the next year working with a developmental psychologist and a program development specialist to create what is now known as The Empowerment Space. The name, The Empowerment Space, was chosen to emphasize the need for a program that used skills to empower children to heal from bullying, and to give them the tools and space in which to do this. The vision for the Empowerment Space is to help educate communities with children at a crisis point of bullying between ages 10-18, and to provide individual sessions for coping strategies and self-esteem building skills, to truly empower kids to heal from their own pain of bullying. The hope is that the program I created will be taken to other communities across the country, that it will show more success for children to really increase their positive self-esteem and coping strategies. All of this is designed to be done with the support of their families and school, to decrease the effects from bullying behaviors.

Pulling all the concepts together into a transformation

We've covered the core concepts of empathy, empowerment, and engagement, as well as the healing tools of positive self-talk, positive bystanders, and coping mechanisms. How can we pull all of them into a plan that will transform our relationships with our children?

Let me show you how I, as a family therapist, implement this with my own clients. Then, we can talk about how you can bring these concepts into your own family's daily life.

The Empowerment Space is a 10-week cognitive behavioral program addressing coping skills and self-esteem skills with children. Each week there are new activities that will be completed through role plays, activity book assignments, and learning cognitive behavioral skills. We teach children that through their own words and behavior, through cause and effect, they can change their own situations around bullying.

In our first session together, we go through an assessment with the child and parents, so that we can fully understand the type of bullying, the extent of bullying, and how the child feels about the treatment session.

In our second session, we start with a quick assessment, called the Multi-Dimensional Peer Victimization Scale (MVPS), which just helps us to keep tabs on incidents of bullying and how the child is feeling that week (self-esteem, self-talk, and coping). We talk about how our bodies react to bullying. Instinctually, when we feel threatened, we experience either a fight, flight, or freeze response. It's important that the child understands there's a physical response of adrenaline and cortisol in the body. We also talk about the mental, emotional, and relational effects of bullying, so that the child starts to feel that his or her experience is normal and manageable.

In our third session, we learn how to role play. We practice what it will look like and feel like to interact with a bully, how to talk to the bully, how to calm yourself with breathing, and how to cope with the feeling of being threatened in the moment. We role play different types of bullying: physical, verbal, relational, and cyberbullying. We also talk about positive and negative bystanders.

In our fourth session, we assess the previous week's bullying with the MVPS scale, and we talk about positive self-talk. We come up with a list of positive attributes that the child thinks she embodies. We think of what her parents, teachers, and friends would say are her positive attributes. Then, we role play what positive self-talk and negative self-talk sound like, in the moment. We also discuss what high self-esteem and low self-esteem look like.

We also plan the first school meeting that we'll have with the parents and the child. We aim to have a school meeting between the fourth and fifth sessions. In that school meeting, we ask for a vice principal, or at least a teacher, to be in the room with us. We talk about the types of bullying we think are occurring, what some goals are that we can all work toward, and we make sure we're all using the same terms when we're talking with the children. For instance, positive self-talk when helping the student handle bullying during the school day. It's important that a meeting with the school is extremely collaborative.

In our fifth session, we assess the previous week's bullying with the MVPS scale, and we define assertive, passive, and aggressive communication, and describe what it looks like to challenge social situations. We role play to communicate effectively. The parents then come into the second part of this session, and we talk about the Three Es: empathy, empowerment, and engagement. We practice role play with the parents so that they understand how to communicate with their child about the bullying.

In our sixth session, we assess the previous week's bullying with the MVPS scale, and we talk about how to communicate with a parent about the bullying, using assertive communication skills, and how to know whether it's an appropriate time to reach out to an adult for help. The parents come back in to role play the Three Es again, because the concept is so crucial to the child's success. The child "grades" the parent on how well the parent is using the Three Es at home, an opportunity which the child usually loves.

In our seventh session, we assess the previous week's bullying with the MVPS scale, and we talk about the child's locus of control: what the child has control over and what he doesn't. He has control over what situations he puts himself into, how he reacts to a situation, and how he exits from a situation. We role play different scenarios and what he has power over in each case, to show him that he has more power than he thinks. Through these exercises, he sees that he can choose how he engages with a bully or chooses not to engage, perhaps using positive self-talk, deep breathing, reaching out for help, focusing on positivity and gratitude, or expressing feelings through creative outlets.

Between sessions seven and eight, we have a second school meeting to update everyone on how the bullying is going, and review and fine tune our goals. We don't want to tell the schools what to do because they already feel on the defensive, so we want to be collaborative.

In our eighth session, we assess the previous week's bullying with the MVPS scale, and we learn how to integrate the fight/flight/freeze response, positive self-talk, positive communication skills, the Three Es, and concentrating on the child's focus of control.

In our ninth session, we do a full assessment of the bullying situation so that we can compare the data we gathered back in the very first session. We then role play a situation that helps us to review all the skills we learned throughout our time together.

The tenth session is a graduation party to celebrate the child's progress and positive changes. We have a special dessert and invite the parents, to help the child feel like something has truly changed in her life.

We have our final school meeting to establish an ongoing engagement plan, so that the school will help to keep tabs on the child's bullying situation.

After the ten weeks, we have three follow-up sessions, one month, two months, and three months later. These follow up meetings truly assess whether the changes are long term, and if increased self-esteem and a decrease in bullying have continued.

Typically, after these follow-up sessions, the bullying has decreased, the child feels empowered, and the child and the parent have grown closer together.

True transformation from empathy, empowerment, and engagement

Angela's story really shows the power of the full Empowerment Space process.

I walked into the waiting room one day to get my client for the first session for The Empowerment Space Program. She was a 13-year-old, depressed female who was being cyberbullied at school. I had a brief conversation with the mother Suzanne before the first session to assess whether her daughter Angela met criteria for the pilot study.

Suzanne, Angela's mother, reported that the cyberbullying had been going on for the last year. It had started as a joke and this group of girls had been Angela's friends. Then, slowly over the past year these peers, they started leaving Angela out and ignoring her, ostracizing her at school, and finally spreading rumors about her, that she had engaged in sexual activity with a boy who attended her school.

Angela's mother Suzanne found out from Angela's Social media page that for months this group of girls had been relational bullying her on a daily basis, and making mean comments on social media about her. Angela was isolating herself in her room more, and seemed depressed and not interested in going to school. This, coupled with the Social media comments, made Suzanne worry and speak to her daughter. Eventually, she called me.

Suzanne felt hopeless and helpless watching her daughter go through the bullying. Every day, she saw her daughter's anxiety before going to school. It had gotten so bad that Angela was losing weight and would sometimes throw-up before school would start.

Suzanne was a single mother and Angela's father was not in the picture. He had been gone for many years now. Suzanne was raising her daughter all by herself.

During the first session I had with Angela, I saw how depressed she felt. At times during our sessions, she would reveal that she had felt like hurting herself but did not have a clear plan, means, or intent.

The first few sessions were about educating both Angela and her mother about bullying and giving them better coping skills to use. Both women appeared very beat down by the circumstances of the bullying and had no idea what to do. Both mother and daughter felt powerless.

It was after the first school meeting, four weeks into the program, that I began to see a sliver of hope. Angela came into the session telling me she had been able to use her positive self-talk to help her better handle some of the comments others were saying, able to assure herself that what was being said about her was not true. She expressed understanding of the idea that she had control over how she reacted to her situation and felt more comfortable managing her reactions when the other girls would taunt her.

In the school meeting, it was noted that Angela had started engaging more with other children, both in the classroom and during recess. The teachers noted seeing her isolate less and engage more with a different group of girls. Suzanne, Angela's mother, was hopeful and the rest of the meeting was spent working on goals for follow-up by the next school meeting.

Two weeks later, Angela came for her eighth session with a smile on her face. This was the first time in eight weeks that I had seen her smile.

I started asking questions about how the bullying had gone the week before and Angela spoke up, stating that she had made a new friend. This new friend was not in the same clique as her other peers. She had gotten to know her working on one of her projects in class. Angela was very hopeful that this would blossom into a new, close friendship, but she was cautious and taking the friendship slowly.

By week ten, both Angela and Suzanne were doing better. Angela was learning new coping skills in the program to handle any further bullying with the girls at school. She was starting to isolate less, have more plans on the weekend with different friends, and her appetite increased. Angela had not spoken of having any suicidal thoughts since week four.

Suzanne had been working hard in the program on learning how to effectively use empathy, empowerment, and engagement with her daughter to continue to address the relational bullying. Suzanne felt more confident in her own abilities to use the Three Es, felt she had a better handle on things, and felt much more powerful.

The school and Angela's mother had developed a nice, collaborative approach centered around communication. Things were not perfect, but Suzanne felt that the school was listening to her and trying to help her daughter.

Angela would come to sessions once per month for the next three months. Angela would check in and fill out paperwork to measure the change in bullying level with her peers. Each month, she reported less and less bullying, as well as increased development of more positive friendships, with girls who were kind and who valued her for who she was.

Suzanne felt that communication at home was getting better, and Angela was more readily coming to her mother when an issue came up at school. Angela was having friends over again, had tried out for a play at school, and had actually got the lead role.

By week thirteen, the final week of the program, the bullying had pretty much stopped. Angela was better able to cope when she had encounters with mean peers, and Suzanne was better able to communicate about these issues, allowing mother and daughter to become closer.

The final session arrived. Suzanne and Angela were in the waiting room. They both had smiles on their faces. I brought them both in and asked the final batch of questions to measure progress. Suzanne turned to me and said that things were getting better with Angela, she felt much closer to her, and had more of an authentic relationship with her daughter. Angela agreed and smiled again.

Suzanne explained that having an approach like the Three Es and the thirteen weeks of the program taught her how to really communicate effectively with her daughter. Suzanne turned to me and, with tears in her eyes, said, "Thank you." Angela then gave me a big hug, and they said goodbye.

There is no amount of money that can replace the knowledge that you, as a therapist, have made a difference in the life of a child who had been thinking about killing themselves. It is a moment of bliss, rarely experienced as therapists, that the work we do really can change a person's whole life. I turned back to write my final progress note and started to tear up for affecting another person so strongly and deeply.

What does a child's life look like *after* experiencing the Empowerment Space?

Perhaps the best way to show how empathy, empowerment, and engagement can change a child's and a family's life forever, is to describe for you what's happened to Lauren and her parents.

After the heated graduation session, I felt sad. I felt that Lauren was robbed of the chance to really enjoy her progress in the program and the positive changes that were made and spoken about by her teachers. Lauren was certainly being bullied less and was coping better, but we weren't at the finishing point I wanted, the one that Lauren and her family deserved.

I wanted to bring the family back for another session. I called Lauren's father, Rob, and he explained to me that Lauren needed a break from the program for a while. He stated there was no need for a corrective graduation session. He felt the work was done for now. I strongly encouraged the importance of this session but I also did not want to push past the families' limits. I encouraged them to come back in within a month to follow-up, in order to finish the pilot program. He said that he would and appreciated my help. We came up with a tentative date for the next session.

I was looking forward to our meeting and excited to process out Lauren's feelings and try to help the family. On the day of the meeting, when I saw Lauren and her dad sitting in the waiting room, I was happy they had come. Linda did not make this session. I first had Lauren come in. I asked her how she felt after the last session. She said it had been hard for her, as she doesn't like it when her parents are angry with her. But she felt that the session had allowed her an opportunity after they'd left to really share her frustration with her mother and father, with how they'd acted in the session.

She started to cry as she explained to me what she'd said to her parents. Lauren felt that the session had allowed her an opening to be honest with her parents and tell them how bad she felt every time they got frustrated with her. She told them that the way they spoke to her left her feeling worse, and not better. Lauren explained that confronting them had been a cathartic experience for her. She felt this was the first time her parents had really listened to her and respected her opinion. Lauren explained that when she was speaking to her parents, she really tried to use a lot of the positive self-talk that she'd learned in the program.

I sat there and listened to this story Lauren was telling me. I was blown away by the courage she had to speak to her parents and let them know how she was feeling. I felt this was the first step in the right direction. I told Lauren how proud I was of her. She gave me a smile and told me she was actually proud of herself this time.

I could not believe what progress was made within the ten weeks. I thought the last session hadn't gone well, but to my surprise, it had led to this amazing conversation with her parents, and Lauren allowing her voice to be heard.

And Maggie, too, has found her own voice.

Maggie and her mother, Shannon, were able to make increasing headway on their relationship using the Three Es, and the relational bullying had almost stopped. By the last session at week thirteen, Shannon told me she had some important news to share.

I brought Maggie in for the session and I started asking about any bullying that had taken place the week before. Maggie looked at me with a big smile and stated that things were "SO much better" and that she was super happy. The girls who teased her were far from her mind. She was feeling better and had made new friends.

Then, this bigger smile came to her face. She told me there was this cute boy who had stood up for her once when she was being bullied by the girls she'd thought were her friends. She had forgotten about the tall, dark-haired guy because at the time she'd been so distraught.

It was the end of the school year and this guy that Maggie described as "cute" came up to her. He turned to her and gave her the biggest compliment. He told her that he was so impressed by how strong she'd been this year. He'd seen from the beginning how mean these other girls had been towards her, and how she'd stood strong and shown that what they did would not bother her.

He asked if he could just give her a big hug. Maggie did not know what to say. She had tears in her eyes because someone actually noticed her strength and courage at school and praised her—never mind someone as cute as he was.

Maggie was blown away by the compliment that this cute boy had given her. She went home and shared the conversation with her mother.

How can you bring the Empowerment Space into your family?

If you'd like to bring these principles into your own family, I'd recommend that you use our ten-week plan as a guideline for your conversations with your child and your school. Start by speaking empathically with your child and truly listening to her. Then, slowly introduce how to use positive self-talk. Empower your child by showing him that he does have some amount of control in their bullying situation, even if it's just focusing on his breathing or how he reacts. Set up monthly meetings with the school, and speak collaboratively with the faculty about how to address the bullying. Don't seek to tell him what to do, but truly engage with them in creating a plan together.

Every child and every family will have a different reaction to empathy, empowerment, and engagement, but the framework is simple enough and flexible enough to help everyone through a difficult bullying situation and, ultimately, to help your child feel seen, heard, and loved.

My success story

The difference between my fourth-grade self, so hurt by that group of girls who made me feel invisible and worthless, and my fifth-grade self is remarkable. I have new friends. I've begun to feel confident in myself and my emotions. My teacher even gives me compliments, and I am thriving in school. I've started to believe that I am worthy as a person, and that not every person is out to get me. I've started to relax and make plans with friends again. I have started to make some friendships that even to this day are still in my life.

This is the very last day of the year. I actually have made some solid friendships and am excited for the summer to come and kids to play with. We are having our party in the room. There are food and drinks to enjoy the celebration. Then, my teacher interrupts our celebration to present the prestigious Student of the Year award. He stands up, clears his throat, and smiles. The entire class gets quiet, their eyes on him.

The next thing I know my name, Danielle Targan, is called! Yes, my name is called as the Student of the Year. My teacher has chosen me as the best because in his eyes I demonstrated everything right about being a good student and good person. I am elated and start to tear up, but this time it's happy tears. My year of change and determination to try again after a horrible year of depression and bullying has been a success. I feel vindicated. These tears of joy are not only because my teacher sees who I am, but also because of my peers. They are all happy for me (maybe even a bit envious) and their happiness shows in their smiles, kind words, and body language. I know they think this is a truly well-deserved reward.

I go home to tell my mother the good news and I think I see a tear in her eye when she finds out. Maybe she is happy that after my year of complete depression and sadness, the sun is finally beginning to shine for me.

I can't help thinking in the back of my mind that this means an end to the bullying. You see, once bullying stops, it doesn't mean it won't happen again. I am going into my sixth grade and final year of elementary school. The worry is still in the back of my mind. But for once I can say, I am finally able to breathe a sigh of relief, at least for this one day. I feel like I am truly on top of the world and this feels damn good!

Epilogue

Los Angeles 2017

In writing this book, I have undergone a great deal of self-reflection, as I look back on my own personal experiences from a much earlier time in my life when I was deeply pained. I sit here today and hope that I have made an impact on parents' abilities to feel that they have the roadmap and some guidance to really utilize the Three Es of empathy, empowerment, and engagement to speak to their children about bullying.

I hope that I have given useful tools and examples of dialogue to help parents who may be feeling powerless as they struggle with the issue of constant bullying.

I think back to how my story ends. I finished my sixth-grade year successfully and with a great new group of friends, friendships which I'd fostered slowly over the year. I was then told by my mother that we were moving school districts. I was going to have to start all over again meeting new friends. I would not be accompanying my grammar school friends into middle school.

I was worried at first that the change in school districts would be very hard and I would not meet a good and kind group of friends. All my old thoughts and fear rose up inside me.

Looking back, I am proud of how tall I stood that first day at a new junior high. I knew I was not alone as I insisted on remaining connected with my grammar school friends. I started to slowly meet new friends in middle school and gain regular connections. There were a lot of ups and downs in meeting new people and seeing over time who I would truly connect with.

It did take until my third and final year of middle school to truly develop a strong group of friends. I endured bullying at times during those years with a group of boys in a biology class. This same group would sit near me every day and call me the most horrific names. I remember clearly as if it was yesterday, sitting in the classroom surrounded by this group of middle school boys telling me I was "ugly," "fat," and "lame."

I remember that pain as vividly today as if it just happened. I felt so humiliated, and all the teacher did was ask them to stop, day after day. There was no awareness then of how their cruel comments would affect me, or of the darkness I felt.

My mother would still be a support system and help me deal better with the boys' cruel comments. But the lingering feeling that I was ugly and unwanted as I was growing into an adolescent woman had an impact on my self-image.

I continued to go to high school and met even more wonderful female friends. However, I was teased in the eleventh grade in a humanities class by another group of male peers. I remember having the same feelings of inadequacy that I'd felt back in the fourth grade and the eighth grade.

The teachers all responded with asking the boys to stop making their mean comments, but nobody really thought about how hurtful their statements were. No one thought about how it would affect my growth in adolescence. I did not date much and was definitely a late bloomer.

My self-esteem was shattered from the bullying I experienced every few years throughout my childhood. I did not feel pretty and suffered from a low self-esteem. However, although I had a low self-esteem in some areas, I managed to make wonderful connections with friends. I was a very good friend to others and I knew the value and importance in how much friendship meant to me.

Over the years, if a friend disappointed me, I would feel raw pain. Other friends or family tried to protect me, advising me not to invest so heavily in my friends, not to expect so much.

But my friends were the people who saved me and helped me get through adolescence. The connections and good people I met changed my entire life. My friends helped me find myself and discover that the qualities I brought to the table were valued. As a teenager, your friends' opinions matter more than anything.

I found as I got older that I needed to attend therapy to address my childhood bullying. Those past experiences had hugely affected me as a young adult. I struggled to develop healthy relationships with men, and my negative self-esteem was continuously being triggered by various issues.

As I look back on those challenging years when I was bullied, I wish there had been more understanding of what bullying was, how serious it was, and how to effectively deal with it. I think of the book I have written today and hope that parents now have more useful tools. I hope that they will use these tools to take the courageous step to help better support their own children to move into a safe place, with less depression and a higher degree of self-worth.

There is more known today and more practical steps taken to counter bullying. Thanks to social media, we now have more awareness and less acceptance for cruel behavior.

I think back to my own years of bullying and through my own therapy, I am grateful for the person I have become. I work hard at everything I do. And because of my own experiences of bullying and the pain I endured in school, I can now take my strength and help other, more powerless victims and families.

Every day that I read an article or see a YouTube video of a child asking for help, or one that did not make it, I die a little inside. I feel so powerless some days that I cannot help all families heal from bullying. I never want children to experience such intense pain and anguish that they want to stop living or kill themselves. Yet, we have kids every day, eight years old or even younger, who hurt themselves or commit suicide.

The cruel reality of our world is a daily burden for bullied kids. I am so grateful that I healed many of my own childhood wounds. And yet, I know there are still some days when those fears and painful memories bubble to the surface, and I realize that those memories will be a part of me forever.

However, the determination I have to help families has led me to write this book. It has led me to develop an approach—a guide—that may help other families truly heal from bullying. I am making it my life's mission to be loving, compassionate, and kind to others around me. It is my mission to help as many families as I can to feel that with knowledge, there truly is power for change to happen.

I am not perfect, nor are the Three Es. But I do believe in the work I have conducted with 20 years of experience, that the roadmap provided in this book will help guide families into a happier place with a better sense of themselves.

With much gratitude and love,

Danielle Matthew

What's Next?

It takes time for you to change how you've been thinking, speaking, and acting with your child, and you might need support, as you incorporate the Three Es into your family.

If you would like more information about how you can work with the Empowerment Space to bring empathy, empowerment, and engagement to your family, please visit:

www.empowerment.space

Recap Of The Three Es

EMPATHY

The first step to empathy: listen to your child's feelings without judgment.

The second step to empathy: mirror your child's feelings.

EMPOWERMENT

The first step to empowerment: ask your child about a plan to handle future bullying and create a bullying action plan together.

The second step to empower your child: role play the bullying action plan.

The third step to empowering your child: check in with how your child is feeling about the bullying action plan.

ENGAGEMENT

The first step to engagement: establish a regular check-in with your child.

The second step to engagement: set up a school meeting and agenda.

The third step to engagement: follow up with the school personnel, concerning the discussed interventions.

Glossary
(in order of appearance in the book)

Bullying: a persistent pattern of behavior that happens where someone enforces power over another person, through the threat or use of verbal, physical, or relational violence

Conflict: a one-time fight between two equals

Physical bullying: patterned physical violence toward someone with less power, includes hitting, kicking, punching, or tripping another person

Verbal bullying: patterned verbal violence toward someone with less power, includes name-calling and making mean comments to someone's face

Cyberbullying: bullying that takes place using electronic technology and includes phone calls, text messages, emails, social media posts, blogs, and creating fake websites in someone else's name. The scope of cyberbullying changes as fast as our technologies change.

Relational bullying: ostracizing a person, leaving them out, gossiping or spreading rumors

Re-victimization: in the aftermath of "telling" on a bully, the victim experiences bullying again, either through repeat bullying or through an outsider's harsh reaction toward the victim

Empathy: understanding another person's perspective from their viewpoint

Empath: one who is sensitive to another's thoughts and feelings

Role play: acting out or perform the part of a person in a hypothetical scenario to increase empathy for each other's feelings and perspectives

Mirroring: making a statement that reflects back what the other person is saying or feeling

Empowerment: allowing someone else's voice and ideas to be important

Bullying action plan: the detailed action-steps that your child will take before, during, and after a bullying incident

Engagement: following through with your child's plan to cope with the bullying and consistently checking in with your child, the school, and any other people involved assist in executing that plan

Self-compassion: understanding that you, as a parent, have a hard situation and finding ways to say kind words to yourself without being overly hard or self-critical

Bystanders: people who are in the area when a bullying situation is taking place

Positive bystander: a person who can positively change a bullying situation by not going along with the bully's negative behavior, make the behavior positive, or turn the negative behavior away from the victim.

Negative bystander: a person who can negatively impact a bullying situation by vocally going along with the bully, encouraging mean behavior, or standing with the bully to hurt the victim

Neutral bystander: a person who is not actively negative toward a bullying victim but is also not proactively standing up for the victim, either

Acknowledgements

To the team at Paper Raven Books thank you for your amazing energy, guidance determination and support! Morgan, I am so grateful for you!

To Jennifer Lourie, Tina Pedersen Paddock, Cristina Portillo-Via, Teri Miglin, Julia Robinson, Suzanne Dodson Ranson, Vicky Mirakian, Isabel Stenzel Byrnes, Jennifer Graydon and the late Ana Stenzel.

Thank you for all always supporting me. I am forever grateful to each and every one of you for your unique friendship. I am very blessed to have each of you in my life!

There were too many special friends to name for this book so above are just a few and there are so many more who have touched my life from childhood through adulthood, I am forever grateful to each and every one of you.

To Katie Vernoy for her endless help and support as my business coach and for bringing The Empowerment Space to light. Thank you!

To Carolyn Enenstein for her amazing marketing guidance and friendship through the book process.

To my parents, Cheryl and Nace; Stephan and Janne thank you for all your support and encouragement. Thank you for always telling me how proud you are of me.

To Kirk Smalley, It was an honor to have you write the forward to my book. I feel so blessed to call you my friend. Thank you from the bottom of my heart for coming into my life.

To the late Julie Wilson, I am forever grateful to you for helping me make my passion a reality.

To Gwendolyn Hansen, I would be lost without you. Thanks for always helping me find my way back!

To my Beta Readers, thank you all for taking the time to read the manuscript and lend your feedback. I am so appreciative of each and every one of you.

To my husband, Jaime. Thank you for your ideas, support and help to make the work I do a reality. You have provided love, guidance, and support to me through this whole entire journey. I love you to the moon and back.

Finally, the book is dedicated to the many families out there who have struggled with bullying. I commend each of you for all your strength and determination. May this book bring a sense of comfort for you.

About the Author

Danielle Matthew is a Licensed Marriage and Family Therapist whose lifelong mission is to treat and support bully victims and their families, aid schools and health and wellness professionals, and educate others about the bullying epidemic.

Danielle has worked as a clinician in the field for over 20 years with children and adolescents in various environments including day treatment programs, residential facilities, and outpatient services. She has supervised a therapeutic one-on-one behavioral program, facilitated therapy groups and conducted clinical authorizations for an insurance provider. Danielle has additionally conducted group and individual therapy with adults.

In 2014 as Danielle became concerned by an increase in patients suffering from bullying, she conducted research which concluded that while there are many bullying prevention programs, there are few programs in Los Angeles that address the crisis point of bullying to help children and adolescents heal. In response, Danielle developed The Empowerment Space Bullying Therapy Program to ensure that there is crucial support available to empower children and their parents with skills to address bullying and create stronger, more positive support systems for children.

To further increase bullying awareness and action, Danielle provides numerous presentations to community organizations and schools as well as medical, health and wellness professionals. Danielle is featured on Kids In The House.com and has made guest appearances on podcasts such as The Family Couch, WiseInside, and We Heart Therapy. Danielle routinely presents bully awareness education to Pepperdine University graduate students and to faculty at Cedar Sinai Medical Center, among other organizations.

Danielle treats bully victims in the greater Los Angeles area, and is available for consultations and speaking engagements nationwide.

Made in the USA
San Bernardino, CA
24 October 2017